COFFEE WITH NONNA

Coffee With Nonna

The Best Stories of My Catholic Grandmother

VINCENT M. IEZZI

SERVANT
BOOKS

PUBLISHED BY ST. ANTHONY MESSENGER PRESS
CINCINNATI, OHIO

Published by St. Anthony Messenger Press
28 W. Liberty St.
Cincinnati, OH 45202

Cover design: Alan Furst, Inc., Minneapolis, Minn.

04 05 10 9 8 7 6 5 4 3

Printed in the United States of America
ISBN 1-56955-321-1

Library of Congress Cataloging-in-Publication Data

Iezzi, Vincent M.
    Coffee with Nonna : the best stories of my Catholic grandmother /
Vincent M. Iezzi.
        p. cm.
    ISBN 1-56955-321-1 (alk. paper)
     1. Christian life–Catholic authors. I. Title.
    BX2350.3 .I49 2002
    248.4'82–dc21

                                                                    2001008495

*These stories are dedicated to
my grandchildren—
Kristine, Michael, Robert, David,
Jessica, Giavanna, Eric, and Dominic—
and to all grandchildren*

Contents

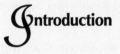ntroduction

"When you are happy, you should talk to God; when you are sad, God needs to talk to you."

Domenica Maria D'Amore

My Nonna was a woman of life.

Whenever I needed a Band-aid to cover the smallest nick from the thorny bush of growing up, I would go to my Nonna. And Nonna would say:

"There once was a wise man who said ..."

"A great man once wrote ..."

"Did you know that one of the great saints said ..."

A story would follow and I would be cured, not because the stories were authentic but because I believed her. My Nonna was the smartest person in my life.

My grandmother didn't have any degrees, but she had the wisdom of a philosopher. Her education was very informal. Her classrooms were God, life, love, family, friends. She would watch and listen to these, and she would take notes.

Imagination and good sense were her elementary education, followed by faith and hope, which were her high school studies, and finally love, concern, and sensitivity, which took her to college. She was of peasant stock, short and plain, but in our family she stood as tall as an ornamented column that supports the roof of the largest cathedral. She possessed the great wisdom of knowing when to talk and when to be quiet, when to add and when to subtract, when to give the whole and when to give a part.

She often told me she learned all things from Jesus. Jesus always spoke to the plain people, she said, those who were plain of heart and simple of ways and humble of mind.

Another time, she told me her greatest wish was to have been an apostle. I remember thinking to myself, *But you're a woman.* Now I know she *was* an apostle in her faithful, uneducated plainness. She was a child just as they were.

I spent a lot of time with Nonna, especially during the War years when she cared for me and my cousins while our mothers worked and our fathers were in the military. Nonna taught me to think and to use my imagination. She made me see and appreciate simple and ordinary things. She directed me to God and helped me see that He was always within reach and could be found in the plain and simple moments. She made me fall in love with being Italian. She tutored me to love and to speak her language. She showed me how to live in a family and how to re-create it for others. She gave me so many gifts to cherish and to share with others.

Through the years I have many times repeated her stories and teachings. As it is with oral tales, I really don't know where she left off and where I added on. These stories are as I remember them and have retold them so often. The only thing that is missing is Nonna and the coffee.

One

The Coffee Makers

The majority of our neighbors were Italians, but we had Irish, Greeks, Polish, Ukrainians, Lithuanians, Jews, and three black families.

In my youth your color or nationality made no difference. What was important was how you acted toward us kids on the block. If we could play in front of your house, if we could sit on your step, or if you gave us a treat for Halloween, then you were our friend and all was OK. Prejudices and discriminations were not part of our kids' world. These were grown-up things.

To my innocent mind, "grown-up" meant being able to do certain things. Being able to smoke or play pool or get a job or have dates or have important opinions were the things that made you a grown-up. I also thought that being able to eat *brasciole* was a grown-up thing.

Brasciole is thin steak rolled around garlic, parsley, black pepper, salt, and grated Italian cheese. Thread is wrapped around the brasciole to hold the contents in place. This little bundle is fried and then added to the gravy (tomato sauce) to give the gravy extra flavoring.

Brasciole was expensive and hard to get during the War because of the War food rations. The rule in our household was that only the working people in the family could eat it. Now, simply eating brasciole was not the grown-up thing; it was the idea of being able to unwrap the brasciole, to free it of its thread—now, that was being grown-up!

Another thing that I believed was a grown-up thing was being able to drink coffee. At a young age I was permitted to drink coffee—or what I believed was coffee—and of course that made me halfway grown-up. This grown-up act was granted to me because early morning coffee was my grandmother's time. She liked to sit and drink her coffee, peacefully, quietly, with no complications.

Years later I realized this was her time of prayer and her time for deep thinking and planning for the day ahead. She knew if I didn't sit and have coffee with her, she would have no peace or quiet or time for thoughts. I would have been pestering, questioning, and above all nagging her for coffee because I had been born with a strong love for this beverage. So she was wise and granted my wish, but only if I acted like a grown-up—that is, peaceful and quiet. (I also realized later that what I believed was coffee was Nonna's watered-down coffee.)

Now, down the street from us in a row house just like ours was a black family. This family had two daughters who were mutes, Alma and Bernice, and often they would sit on their step signing to each other and making loud unfamiliar sounds that frightened me. They always seemed so angry and so upset every time they talked. When my grandmother saw them, she would simply smile and nod her head, and they would do the same to her. If I were walking past their house with my grandmother, I would tighten my hold on her hand and crouch as close as possible to her, because, as I said, they frightened me.

It goes without saying that I avoided these two girls at all costs, always.

One day, while I was playing in our street, my grandmother called for me from the front door of our house. I began running to her, passing the house of the two mutes. The girls were sitting on the steps signing to each other and making those loud funny sounds. I bolted into the street to avoid the pavement in front of their house.

Nonna saw this. I ran into the house, and she followed me in. Moments later as she was cooking, she asked in Italian, "Why did you run in the street when you passed those nice ladies, Alma and Bernice?"

"I don't like them," I said.

"Did they ever hurt you or anyone you know?" she asked carefully.

"No. I just don't like them."

"You never 'just don't like' people. Did you ever talk to them?"

I laughed. "Nonna, they don't talk. They're dumb, and they make funny loud noises."

She continued with her cooking.

"Would you like a cup of coffee?"

"I had a cup this morning."

Without a thought to my words, she took two cups from the metal cabinet, placed them on the porcelain kitchen table, and poured the coffee.

"Get the milk and sugar, and come sit with me."

We sat and prepared our coffee; she stirred hers for the longest time. I watched her hands. They were so much older than the rest of her. I always thought they were so miraculous because they did good and big things, but they also made me sad because they had been worked so hard.

The aroma of the coffee filled the small kitchen.

"You like coffee, don't you?"

"Yes, Nonna, you know that."

"That's good. It a grown-up thing to drink coffee, and it always gives you and me time to be just us. Understand?"

"Yes, Nonna."

"But always remember that when you enjoy something, it is because others have given it to you out of love. You enjoy life because God gave it to you out of love. You enjoy *pizzelles* because I bake them out of love. How do you think we get coffee?"

"From Brazil and coffee beans." I was so smart.

"Maybe, but who knows for sure? More important is, who knows the recipe for making coffee beans into coffee? Someone has to know how to make good use of the beans so that we can have good coffee, right?"

"Well, you make good coffee."

"No," she said, tightening up her mouth and shaking her head. "There are people who do it better and some that make the very best coffee. Wise men have learned that making the very best coffee is a great secret that is shared by God with only a very few people."

She lifted the cup to her lips and gently sipped.

"You see those two nice ladies, Alma and Bernice. Do you know why they make signs and noises? It is because they are talking about how to make good coffee, the very, very best coffee. Now, because God wanted this to be a secret, He hid His recipe in a language that is hard for all to understand. Those girls are not dumb; they are smarter than you and I. They know the secret of making better coffee." She took another sip of her cup, and there was an air of satisfaction in her eyes.

"Grandma, do you mean they know how to make better coffee than all the people in the rest of the world?"

She nodded her head.

"You mean God told them?"

She again nodded her head.

"You mean those girls are the only ones who know the secret?"

She again nodded her head as she got up from the table and went to the kitchen sink to wash her cup. She returned to her cooking.

I sat at the table alone and amazed.

"I'm going to learn how to make good coffee," I said aloud with great conviction.

Several weeks later, a peddler came to our front door selling shoelaces. He gave out a small card that had the alphabet in the hand signs. I knew then that God wanted me to learn how to make good coffee, or this man would never have come to our house. I gave him a nickel, took the card, went to my room, and began to learn.

Weeks later as I was walking down the street, Alma and Bernice were on their front steps, their hands moving rapidly, unintelligible sounds pouring excitedly from their mouths. I decided I was going to talk to them. My heart was beating fast, and I was scared. Alma caught my eye, and I immediately signed, "Hello."

She let out a yell, and a big smile covered her face.

Oh God, I thought, *I must have done it wrong.*

Soon Alma and Bernice were grabbing me and smiling and signing, "Where did you learn to sign?" They dragged me to their step, and we sat and "talked." I was so very slow with the signs that a lot of times they knew what I was signing before I finished. Yet I was so excited to be talking with them, and they were just as happy. Their sounds were more excited than ever before, although still somewhat frightening to me.

As time went by, I began to sign more quickly, and one day while signing I stopped my usual smiling and began to make inarticulate sounds also. The two girls just stopped and looked at my mouth in shock and confusion. Their faces grew sad. I knew I had done something wrong. I had stepped on hallowed ground. I immediately signed that I was sorry. They smiled, and we were friends again. I knew I would have to wait, but I vowed that someday I would just flatly ask them how to make the best coffee.

Some days later my grandmother saw me sitting with Alma and Bernice on their front steps and signing. She called, and I ran home.

"What were you doing?"

"Talking to my friends Alma and Bernice. They are nice girls, and they are so smart. I'm trying to teach them Italian in their language."

Nonna smiled and hugged me.

"But where did you learn to talk with your hands?"

"From this card." I pulled out my sign language card from my jacket pocket. It was all soiled, torn, and worn to pieces.

"I am so proud of you. See how happy you have made those two ladies? You have become part of their quiet world. This is good. This is very good. You must teach me to say 'Hello' to them."

"I will, Nonna, but you have to learn how to spell first."

"No, I don't, you just show me the hands."

"OK, I will teach you." I went to the sink to wash my hands.

"You know, Nonna, I asked them yesterday how to make good coffee."

The excitement and smile left my grandmother's face. She stood upright.

"And they laughed and made louder sounds. And they started to sign so fast I didn't understand them."

"You must not ask! That is their secret with God. They can't teach you with their hands. The secret is in the sounds they make. God and they alone know what those sounds mean."

I immediately realized that this was why, weeks before, when I tried to imitate their sounds, Alma and Bernice had looked so sad. Now I would never know how to make the best coffee. I was very disappointed, and Nonna knew it.

"Don't be sad," she said. "You have made new friends, and you will never be frightened by them again. You are closer to God, and that is good, right?"

"But how do people get to know how to make good coffee?"

"Your friends will talk to God for you, and He will send you the knowledge, you'll see. God will do this because you have done a good thing. Now teach me. Teach me how to talk to these nice ladies."

"OK," I replied with much excitement and pride, for I was teaching the greatest teacher in my life something she did not know.

About three weeks later my grandmother and I were walking down the street, returning from the Italian grocery store. Alma and Bernice were sitting on their steps. My grandmother smiled, put the grocery bags on the fender of a parked car, turned to them, and signed, "Hi."

The girls were shocked, and with great enthusiasm and excitement they signed, "Hello."

"What did they spell?" my Grandmother asked.

"They said, *'Ciao.'*"

Nonna retrieved the grocery bags from the car, fighting back tears. She reached for my hand, tightly held it, turned to the surprised ladies, nodded, and proudly walked home.

This same conversation continued on for years, sometimes daily.

Many, many years later, a friend of mine said to me, "My God, this is great coffee. How did you learn to make coffee this good?"

I smiled, then gave out a loud inarticulate noise and said, laughing, "I had two friends who asked God to tell me."

$\mathcal{T}$hose Who Had To Know Knew

One day my grandmother and I were sitting in the kitchen talking about saints. She mentioned her favorites, which included St. Anthony, St. Joseph, St. Raphael, and of course, "Lo Santo," which was her name for St. Francis of Assisi. I, not wanting to be outdone, named all the archangels as my favorites, as well as St. Vincent.

"But, of course, Mary is the greatest," she said with finality.

"Well, I don't always like Mary," I said with conviction.

"What!" Grandmother yelled. This one word bounced off the walls and seemed to run around the small kitchen.

You did it now, I thought. *When will you ever learn to shut your mouth?*

"Why?" The piercing word came from her mouth and echoed in my ears.

"Well,..." I stalled, hoping to give myself some time.

"Well, I am waiting. Why do you not like *la Madonna?*"

"I said I didn't like her *always.*" I was hoping this would minimize whatever punishment I had earned.

"And why not always?" Nonna insisted.

"Well,... I don't understand her," I blurted out.

"What do you have to understand? She was a woman." Her voice lowered and she softly added, "A mother."

"I know that. It's just that she always seemed so calm. She never ... ever got excited. She was so quiet. Well,... like, why didn't she get excited when the angel came to her? Why didn't she get excited about the Baby Jesus?"

There. My feelings about Mary were out. I had made a good point, so I folded my arms across my chest and sat back in triumph.

"Tell me more."

Boy, she is tough. She isn't going to be satisfied, I thought.

"Well ... when she had the Baby Jesus in her belly, why didn't she tell everyone? What was the big secret? When someone in our family is having a baby, we celebrate. I think Mary should have celebrated." My immediate urge then was to get up and run, but this was not to happen, because my grandmother got up from the table first and in one step was standing over me.

"You know, Vinzee, you try to think for God. Don't you know that this was not the way God wanted it to be?"

"But she should have told somebody."

"The people who had to know knew."

"Like Joseph?" I said with a touch of sarcasm.

"Yes, and his family, maybe his brothers and sisters. Mary's mother and father, St. Ann and St. Joachim, knew, and her sisters and brothers and even St. Elizabeth. They all knew. Who else had to know? The time for others would come later."

"That's not fair. The Baby Jesus was there for the whole world, not just for St. Joseph and those others. I know I would have told everybody."

"But she wasn't like you. She understood. Besides, the other world knew."

"The other world? You mean the devil?"

She looked surprised. I don't think she expected that from me, or maybe she had not thought of it herself, but she recovered quickly.

"Oh, I'm certain he knew. But no, I meant the animals. They knew. The angels told them. One of the great saints wrote a book about it, and it is a good story."

She went to the icebox to get the bag of string beans she was hoping to cook that night. She carried the big brown bag back to the table and ripped it open. The beans spilled onto the porcelain tabletop.

"Tell me the story, Nonna."

She smiled. "If I can remember it. Here, help me clean the string beans."

She divided the beans between us and purposely let a few suspenseful moments pass.

"Now I remember. This great saint said that Mary at first was unhappy at the fact that no one knew. After all, this was God's Son, and the Jews had waited for *centuries* for His coming. Why shouldn't they know, and why shouldn't God be praised? But as time passed, Mary came to understand God's will, and once again she made God's way her way. Always remember: When a mother has good thoughts, her baby hears those thoughts; and when the baby is born, the baby will always have those good thoughts."

She started to clean the string beans, pleased that she had made an important point.

"Is that really true, Nonna?"

"Of course," she quickly replied. "That is why Jesus understood God's will. He made His Father's way His way. Because of His mother's thinking these thoughts, Jesus grew up wanting always to do the will of His Father. Remember, He said almost the same words in the Garden that Mary had said many years before."

She leaned back on her heels, satisfied that she had once again made her point.

"Well, anyway, Mary was a little unhappy. She continued to do the housework, and Joseph had told her that she was to rest every day from noon until three o'clock. So each day, after Mary had finished her work, she would go and sit outside in the backyard of the house.

"One morning she was praying to God and asking Him to help her become stronger. After all, to be a mother is a big responsibility, but to be the Mother of God—that was even bigger. Soon an angel came and told her she would be the strongest woman in the world and others would love her for her strength.

"After the angel left, Mary began to hear little sounds. They were like tiny horns tooting. She looked down and saw that a small flower in her garden had opened up its petals and was tooting a soft trumpet call. She understood that the world's knowledge of her Son was to be like these flowers, soft and quiet, and that only those who had to hear would hear. So Mary smiled.

"Remember, Vinzee, thinking things out and understanding what your thoughts are always makes you smile.

"Well, just then she looked up and saw the biggest and most powerful lion—the King of the Beasts—walking toward the house. She wanted to call St. Joseph because the size of this animal frightened her. Instead, she placed her hand on her stomach and calmly sat back in her chair. The lion now began a fast trot, and within moments he was in the yard!

The lion stopped some distance from Mary but directly in front of her. He bowed down and then rested on the grass. Mary smiled. The big lion just sat there in front of Mary, without ever moving, until three o'clock. Then he got up, bowed again to her and the Baby Jesus, and backed away.

"The next day the biggest elephant you ever saw came into the yard. He came the same way the lion had—first walking, then trotting. He also stopped in front of Mary, bowed, and sat on the grass, just as the lion had done the day before. And at three o'clock the elephant left.

The next day a giant bear came. The following day a powerful eagle, and the two days after that, a big fish and a big tall reindeer with great big horns. Each day thereafter, an animal came to the backyard in the same way and did the same thing, and each would leave at three o'clock. This continued day after day, all during the time that Mary was carrying the Child Jesus, until a representative of all the animals in the world had come to see her and bowed down to their King."

"Wow!" I said, breaking the hypnotic state I was in. "Didn't anybody else see these animals coming?" I asked.

"No. Just Mary, the Baby Jesus, and God the Father."

"You mean all the animals in the world came?"

"Well, mostly all. All except five, but they had a special reason for not coming. They had a message to give."

"What were the five animals? What were the messages?"

She thought for a moment. "I'll tell you some other time."

"Oh, Nonna!" I shouted in disappointment.

"The beans are all cleaned. I have to cook now. Later."

It was over. I knew it.

"One more question," I said timidly.

She nodded. She knew she had to compromise or I would bother her into unkindness.

"Was Mary excited about this?"

"Of course she was! She was so pleased that she prayed to God and asked Him to bless all the animals for their actions."

"And was Jesus happy also?" I was pushing it.

"It pleased Him, and it also made Him happy, and it pleased God the Father. In fact, God the Father was so pleased that He made a promise to all the animals in the animal kingdom. He promised that no animal would take part in the crucifixion of His Son. That is why you never hear of any animals being on Calvary."

She walked to the sink.

"Now go. You got two questions for the price of one. If I let you, you will question me to death."

She turned to walk away, and as she went she shouted back, "Oh, do you remember those little flowers that tooted? Well, God made a promise to those flowers that they would be at Jesus' second birth. So on Easter Sunday, the tomb that Jesus was in was almost covered with these little flowers, and when the tomb blew open they tooted and sounded like loud giant trumpets. Do you know what we call those flowers?"

"No."

"Morning Glories," she shouted back to me.

For weeks thereafter and then into months, I tormented my grandmother for the identity of the five animals that had not gone to adore Jesus in Mary's belly.

She held fast with the promise to tell me later. When I now think of this time, I am certain she didn't have the names of the animals and was really working up to them.

Finally the time was ripe.

It was after Christmas. It was a cold, snowy day, a Saturday morning. Nonna came into my room and woke me up.

"Vinzee, come with me to Mass."

On Saturday? But of course. I knew if I didn't go with her she would walk ten city blocks all by herself. Up I got and sleepily dressed myself.

Outside the cold wind woke me. We walked in silence. It was too cold to open our mouths. Finally we arrived at King of Peace, but the inside of the church was just as cold as outside. We never had heat in our church, and as a result parishioners never fell asleep in the winter during any of the Father's sermons.

After Mass Nonna again wanted to see Fr. Casago's Christmas crib. We prayed a few prayers, and finally she spoke.

"Vinzee, what do you see?"

What did I see? I saw a wonder! Father's crib always was a wonder.

"Look around. What animals do you see?"

"There's the cow and the donkey." To get a better look I got up on my tiptoes to see more. "There's a lamb."

"Two more. You just need two more."

"Two more? Why just two more?" I asked, as I continued to look. And then I remembered. Ahh! The five animals!

"There. There's a dog next to one of the shepherds."

"Just one more," she said. I knew she was smiling.

I excitedly looked around Bethlehem. Just one more. I looked hard, but there were no others animals to be found.

"Look far off," Nonna instructed.

I stretched my neck. There in the far distance, a camel!

"The camel."

"Yes, yes. The five animals that did not come to see Mary when she was pregnant. They had to be at Bethlehem."

I fell back on the heels of my snow boots and relaxed my strained legs and stretched neck muscles.

"Come, hot coffee, bread, and butter for breakfast."

I followed her out of our church, and again we walked in silence. I was as happy as possible, for I had finally found out the five special animals. Nothing else was needed, the story was over, or so I thought.

Over coffee, curiosity emerged from my happiness, so I asked. "Why the cow, the donkey, the dog, the lamb, and the camel? They are dopey animals. I would have picked bigger ones, like a horse instead of a donkey, or an elephant instead of a funny camel. Why them?"

"Because they each had something to say to the world from the crib. They also tell the story of Jesus' life. The cow was picked because Jesus was to feed his people. The donkey was there because the donkey is a beast of burden, and Jesus was to carry the burden of our sins. The dog, because he was obedient and a friend to mankind, just as Jesus was to be a friend to all. The lamb had to be there because Jesus was the Lamb of God. And finally the camel was there because Jesus' words would travel far all over the world. So these five animals help tell the Christmas story."

She took a sip of her coffee, looked at me, smiled, and continued.

"Mary knew all these things and kept them to herself. You see, she never had to tell anybody. She didn't have to shout it all over the place. She just was happy because she knew."

Nonna got up from her chair and walked behind me. Softly she touched my head and rested her hand there a few moments.

"When we come to know things from God, we become just like Mary. We become calm and still. Nobody else has to know."

She went to the cabinet and got the bread for breakfast.

Many years later, in prayers of silence, meditation, and eventually contemplation, I came to know things from God, and I never would shout about them for they were mine. They were meant only for me and Him. Who else had to know?

Three

We Are Not All Perfect!

The pastor of our small parish was Fr. Eugene Casago. No priest I knew or would ever know was like him. He was the first priest I ever admired. I admired him not because I thought he was holy—I was too young at the time to know about such things—but because he was a priest who did nice things for my poor parish church. He made our faith exciting in a way that electrified our imaginations and made us more devout.

Above all else he was a showman. He decorated our church for Christmas and Easter as no other priest could do. Yet, in all the splendor and wonder that he created, there was a simplicity, a touch of plain beauty.

Off to the side of the main church was a large chapel that served as a repository for statues. For at least two months before Christmas, Fr. Casago would drape the chapel entrance and begin his secret creation, his Christmas wonder. On Christmas Eve the entire chapel, which as I said was rather large, was open to the parishioners. And there we saw the town of Bethlehem, the countryside around this tiny town, and the cave where Christ was born. The statues nearest us were life size, and the other statues diminished in size with distance. There were plush green pastures, a small reflecting lake, a trickling brook, small rolling hills, and a range of large snow-capped mountains far from the cave and the Baby Jesus.

Near the stable were the busy townfolk, walking to and from their houses. In the distant fields were the resting shepherds sleepily watching their many sheep, and further off could be seen the approaching Magi caravans. The ceiling of the chapel, which was the dark blue sky, was sprinkled with twinkling stars, clean white fluffy clouds, and floating angels of all sizes.

At Easter time no church was "fixed" as nice as King of Peace. The Holy Thursday repository was a wonder of lights. Every candle and candelabra that Father could find was burning before the repository, and every spotlight and lamp was placed around it. White and yellow flowers of many varieties surrounded the Blessed Sacrament, creating an array of bright gold and pure white royalty in divine repose. People came from all the other parishes and even non-Catholic churches in the neighborhood just to see this breathtaking beauty.

Father was an Italian immigrant who spoke Italian primarily, who had a touch of the old country and its ways. He had a deep devotion to St. Francis of Assisi. He once said he "imported Francis of Assisi to Philadelphia" from his native Italy. He said our city was the perfect place for Francis because it was the "City of Brotherly Love," and Francis was a man of love.

Because Fr. Casago had this devotion to St. Francis, it was no wonder that we had Franciscan nuns in our parish school. The Franciscan Missionary Sisters of the Immaculate Conception, who came from many counties of Ireland and still spoke with Irish accents, instructed a student body of poor Italian children with Italian accents. They added to the

"Casago flair" with their support, encouragement, and dedication.

When the time came for this special priest to celebrate his twenty-fifth year as a priest, the poor parishioners collected money as a gift for him. And I was chosen from among the first graders to present him with the basket of flowers that contained the money envelope. I was the proudest kid in my parish and in my school.

My grandmother was even prouder. She made my white suit by hand-sewing, basting, cutting, measuring late into the night for many weeks.

I, meanwhile, was being rehearsed over and over again, as only Franciscan Sisters can rehearse you—that is, with exactness.

The day of the celebration Mass finally came. I was sparkling clean, with a fresh new haircut, and dressed in my handmade short white pants, white shirt, white tie, white jacket, over-the-calf white stockings, and of course, white shoes. It was a cold day, and in our church cold days were very cold. My uncovered legs were blue.

The church was jammed with parishioners. Nonna was there with other friends and members of my family. I was scared. But all would be perfect, because this was for Fr. Casago and because Sr. Mary Teresina and Sr. Mary Madeline had *rehearsed* me.

The Mass was long. Finally it was my turn to act. I carried the basket up to the altar and to our good Father. It was very heavy. (We had never rehearsed with the basket.) I delivered the present with great relief.

Then, as I turned to return to my seat, I was lost. I forgot

which way to go! To the right? No! To the left? No! I froze.
What was seconds seemed like hours. Everyone saw my mistake! Everyone! Of all the times to be dumb!

On the way home my grandmother talked and talked with
great excitement.

"Oh, what a great day this is for Fr. Casago.... How happy we
should be for him.... He is a good, holy man and should be
thanked by all of us...."

I walked beside her, my hand in hers, silently crying. When
she finally noticed my silence, she also noticed my tears.

"What is wrong?" she asked in Italian.

"I made a mistake. After I gave Father the basket, I was supposed to go to the right side of the altar, instead I went to the
left. I messed everything up. I ruined Fr. Casago's day."

"But nobody knew that."

"Yes, they did. Everyone knew. I ruined everything."

My grandmother knew there was no hope, no arguing. So
she waited.

That night, when my eyes were still red and swollen, she
called me to her side. I knew I was about to be doctored,
because when Nonna had something of great importance to
say to me, she would call me to sit with her.

Now, my grandmother knew about a thousand great and
smart men and women in the world, and among the greatest
of all was Michelangelo. So when she said to me, "Come here,
let me tell you a story about that great man Michelangelo," I
knew I was getting the heavy stuff.

And so the story goes:

"Michelangelo was asked by a great pope to sculpt a statue
of Moses. So Michelangelo drew the statue in his mind over

and over again before he began to put it on paper. And when he put it all on paper, he ripped his drawing up and drew it again. He did this over and over.

"Finally he gathered some men and went to a huge quarry and picked the best piece of marble that was there. He returned to Rome with the marble. For days he sat looking at the marble. Over and over again in his mind he formed the statue. When he knew he had it right in his mind, he put the chisel to the marble.

"Now, the pope was a very demanding man. After all, this was a very special statue—the statue of Moses, the man who had seen the face of God. So the pope from time to time demanded to see what Michelangelo was doing. But Michelangelo would always say, 'No! wait until it is completely finished. Then the entire papal court and the whole world can see it.' So the pope agreed to wait.

"Michelangelo worked hard, and when he had finished the statue he called the pope and the papal court to see his final work. The pope, the cardinals, the bishops, and their many secretaries came into the room.

"Sounds of amazement and surprise echoed in the room as they saw this masterpiece. Many of the clergy fell to their knees in total reverence. The pope walked slowly to the statue. He stood before it, looking up at the huge and beautiful Moses— this masterpiece! He was in awe of the huge statue.

"The face of Moses was so real. His eyes looking off into the distance were fiery and intense. The arms and legs, muscular and strong. Michelangelo had made marble come to life! The pope was chilled with reverence and near tears.

"'Perfect! It is perfect!' the pope shouted. Everyone echoed his thoughts and shouted praises and applause.

"Michelangelo looked at the pope and at the entire papal court that had gathered.

"'Perfect?' he said softly. 'No! Never!' He grabbed his hammer and with great force crashed it down on the right foot of the statue.

"'Nothing should be perfect,' he shouted. 'Nothing that man makes or does is to be perfect. Only what God has made is to be perfect.'"

Nonna paused and wet her lips with her tongue.

"So ... we can never consider ourselves as good as Michelangelo, or better than God, can we?"

That did it! It didn't take me long to realize that my grandmother had made things all right. It was a miraculous healing. Now I realized that perfect is something that belongs to God and is only of God, and there is nothing that I could ever do or make that would be perfect. I could only try.

Many years later, when several of my friends were going to Rome on vacation, I told them this story and suggested that they look at the right foot of Moses, and they would see it was missing. Months later, when they returned, they invited me, my wife, and several mutual friends to their home to see slides and pictures and to hear the stories of Rome.

During the evening I asked them. "Did you see the statue of Moses? And the missing right foot?"

They looked at each other and smiled. They finally said, "Yes, and the right foot was there."

"What! Are you sure?"

"Yes. We even asked the tour guide if they had repaired the foot, and he laughed and told us the foot had never been broken. We told him your story, and he laughed even more. He told us it had never happened."

Oh, Nonna!!!

Four

Some People Just Don't Want to Share God

During World War II one of our neighbor's sons was killed in combat. I remember Albert well because he was something of an idol to me. I used to watch him and the older guys play ball. He once offered to help me become "the greatest second baseman" on our block. Just months before he was drafted he married Laura, a pretty girl across the street.

Laura was a special person to me. She had always treated me with kindness, and she never lorded over me like so many of the older kids did. I used to catch her coming home from school, and I would walk her to her house. This was something nice to do for someone who was nice to me. This practice continued for years. When she finished school and went to work, I would wait for her and at 5:30 every evening would "escort" her home.

When Laura and Al were just beginning to notice each other, she would use me as her "spotter." She often would ask me where Al might be at a given time so that she might "accidentally" walk around to where he was. He would see her—and more importantly, she would see him.

When Al realized that I was Laura's "spotter," he began to use me in the same way. One day in innocence I said to him, "Hey, Al, I'm getting tired of being your spy and tired of delivering messages and notes to you from Laura. Why don't you just kiss her and get it over with?"

He must have taken my advice, because three or four weeks later I saw them sitting on her front steps. Then they started going on dates and holding hands. They eventually got married and lived at his parents' house. They had been husband and wife maybe about eight months when he was drafted into the Army and shipped off to Europe for combat.

I vividly remember the day we were informed of his death. I remember all the cries and screams when the telegram arrived. The entire neighborhood converged on Al's parents' house. I still can recall the care and love and tears our neighbors shared with Al's family. I also remember the concern there was for Laura, who was at work when the telegram arrived.

How was she to be told? Who should tell her? Her mother and Al's mother both agreed: "Let her come home from work. Let her be among her family when she learns."

I was sitting on the step when Laura got off the trolley car and began walking up our street. The street was quiet and empty. I was the only person outside. I sat on the step watching Laura come up the street. Being unsure of myself, and not knowing what to do or say, I got up and went inside the house, just as she was nearing me. It seemed the only thing to do— yes, even the wisest thing to do. I ran into the kitchen and told my grandmother that Laura was just coming home. She immediately sat on one of the wooden chairs in the kitchen, as if exhausted.

"*O Dio mi', Pieta,*" my grandmother whispered, and tears came to her eyes. She made the Sign of the Cross and began to pray.

I asked my grandmother why she was praying.

"Oh, Vinzee, Laura needs courage now. All the courage and understanding she can gather. It is not easy to lose love. I lost it two times, and I know the hurt. We should pray for her."

Just then I heard the screams and yells from down the street, and I saw my Nonna's face tighten. I joined her in prayer. It was the only thing to do.

Months later I saw Laura sitting on the step. It was a warm spring day. I walked over to her and sat with her. She was still wearing her black dress and stockings in mourning. We said some small things to each other, then eventually we grew quiet.

Finally she broke the silence by saying, "I want to thank you, Vince, for all the nice things you did for me. You are part of my warm memories of Albert. You always seemed to be there for me.

"You know, the day that we got the news that Albert had been killed, I knew before I got in the house that something had happened to Albert. I saw you get up and go into the house as I walked up the street. That was not like you. I knew something was wrong. Whatever it was I knew it was bad, so I braced myself. Thank you. You helped me a lot that day."

She began to cry and quickly excused herself and went into her house. I walked slowly home. I walked to the kitchen and told my grandmother what had happened. My grandmother began to cry also.

Now, I was aware that this was a sad time, and I sure was aware of the hurt that had befallen Laura, which was the same sorrow that I saw in Al's family. But what was my grandmother crying about?

"Why do you have to cry, Nonna?"

"Crying is a sign of love, and love is the greatest gift God gave us for each other."

"If it is so great, then why cry? Shouldn't we be happy?"

"People cry when they are happy also, Vincenzo. Because when you are happy, it means someone is showing you love. When you are sad, you cry because love is hurt."

She got up from her chair and walked into the living room for a tissue. *I must be stupid,* I thought to myself, *because I don't understand this stuff.* My Grandmother returned to the kitchen and looked at me hard and long. My stupidity must have been obvious to her.

"You want coffee?" she asked and immediately turned the gas on under the coffeepot.

"Did you know, Vinzee, that crying puts you close to God? Jesus cried, and so did His Father. It is written in the Bible."

Whoa! I didn't remember reading that in school during Bible History.

Nonna smiled, knowing I needed an explanation on this.

"There was a wise Italian teacher who wrote an explanation of the first book of the Bible. When God started to create, everything was in darkness. So He made light, and after that He left the world alone for a while. He went back to his desk and began to think of what He should create next. He was so full of love that He wanted to share that love with someone. You see, love is the only thing God needs, because when You are Love, and God is Love, and You love, You need love back.

"So God became sad and began to cry, and His tears began to fall on the earth. This was the first rainfall, and all the waters of the earth were filled with His tears of loneliness. He then parted the water and made the land.

"Later when He decided to make man, He grew so happy that He again began to cry. Again the water fell on earth, so again He parted the water with His finger and made more land. The land began to crunch up, and that's how mountains were formed. Now, because God made man in His image and likeness, man also was able to cry when he was lonely and sad or when he was happy."

"So when we cry we are imitating God?"

"Yes, and God loves when we imitate Him."

I got up and walked to her and kissed her.

"I love you, Nonna, because you help me so much, because you really are my best friend."

She looked up at me. Tears were again welling up in her eyes.

"You see. I am happy," she said.

I kissed her again and began to walk away, because I too felt tears in my eyes.

"By the way," Nonna said, "the story is true, you know. That is why we have two oceans in the world—because God cried two times—and that is why the ocean water is salty—because they are God's tears, and tears are salty."

Of course, I said to myself, *of course it is true.*

Months later I again was sitting with Laura, who still was wearing black, and I told her this story and the story of my grandmother crying for her the day she learned of Al's death. A year or so later Laura was moving to New Jersey. Before she left the neighborhood for the last time, she came to see my grandmother. They sat in the kitchen for a long time, talking in Italian. I couldn't join them because I was too busy being the "best second baseman" on my block.

I joined them just as Laura was saying her last good-bye. She kissed my grandmother. They both began to cry.

Then Laura kissed me.

I looked at the two of them and innocently said, "Boy, I wish you two would stop crying so much and give the rest of us a chance to get close to God."

They laughed and cried harder.

I went into shock.

Some people just don't want to share God.

$\mathcal{G}$od Created Whispers

Once I broke a friend's confidence. My betrayed friend berated me on the front steps of our house, and Nonna overheard the verbal badgering I was receiving. After this confrontation I quietly went into the house to sulk.

Nonna came into the living room and began moving things about, dusting. Finally she said, "Would you like to have some coffee?"

"Sure, Nonna," I said, knowing that this would give me a chance to tell her about my latest problem.

The minute we sat down Nonna said, "There was a story I always wanted to tell you, and I just now remembered it. My grandmother, who was a very smart woman, told me this story, and she said that it was told to her by a great Italian teacher. I think you should hear it."

She reached over and touched my face, her face filled with sympathy, and I knew that she had overheard the confrontation and was willing to help ease the new problem that had clouded my usually bright world. Then she walked around the kitchen gathering all that would be needed for our coffee time.

"Many years ago there were three Wise Men named Caspar and Melchior and Balthazar. These men were very wise in their own kingdoms, and because they were from different kingdoms they did not know each other. Now, one night they each saw a star in the sky that was different from all the others they had seen, and each of them knew that something new and important was about to happen in the world."

She placed the coffee cups, milk, and sugar on the table. I got the paper napkins and spoons.

"Now, at the same time God in heaven was happy, for His Son was to complete the promise made to the Jewish people. Jesus was going to be born to mankind.

"God called His three chief archangels—Gabriel, Michael, and Raphael—to His throne and told them they were being given a special assignment. They were to go to earth and visit the three Wise Men in their sleep. They were to tell the Wise Men to follow the star, and they were to give each of them a special secret. They were also to instruct the Wise Men that no one was to be told the secret that was being given them. The messages were so great a secret that the archangels were also commanded not to reveal the secret to each other.

"So in obedience that night, Gabriel, Michael, and Raphael visited the three Wise Men in their sleep. They told them to follow the star, and they gave them each the secret they had to know. Gabriel went to visit Caspar. Michael went to visit Melchior. Raphael went to visit Balthazar.

"Now, these dreams disturbed the Wise Men. First, they did not want to follow the special star. Second, they did not understand the messages. And finally, they did not understand why they had been chosen to deliver such strange messages. Yet, with all these doubts, each of the Wise Men gathered his belongings, assembled a caravan, and started following the star.

"Balthazar, who had the farthest to travel, left his kingdom first. On his way he unexpectedly met Melchior and his caravan. They discussed the strange star and decided to continue on their trip together. A short time later they met Caspar and his caravan. The three Wise Men discussed the star and how bright and strange it was, and together the three of them with their large caravans followed the star.

"On their journey they discussed the strange dreams that told them to follow the star. Each told the others that he had a secret message to deliver, but they did not tell each other what the secrets were. When they went to Herod for help, they told him they had secret messages for the 'New King.' Herod tried to get the messages from them, but they refused to tell him. So they left Herod's palace and continued to follow the bright star.

"Finally they came to the place where Jesus was, and each of them bowed down to the Babe. What they did not know was that He was the Son of God, so they gave Him the gifts fit only for an earthly king.

"Melchior gave Jesus gold. He then walked up to the Babe and delivered his secret in the Baby Jesus' ear.

"Next came Caspar, who gave Him frankincense. He, too, walked up to the Baby Jesus and whispered his secret in the Babe's ear.

"Finally came Balthazar, who gave the Baby myrrh. He also walked up to the Baby and softly uttered his secret in His ear.

"After each of the Magi had presented his gift and delivered his message, they received the revelation that this King was to be the kindest and most loved of all kings in all the history of world. They stayed with the Child and His parents for a few days and then returned to their own kingdoms.

"God the Father was so pleased with the Three Wise Men that He again called Gabriel, Michael, and Raphael to Him and said, 'Go down to earth and again visit my servants the Magi, and tell them they can now tell each other the messages they whispered to My Son. Furthermore, promise them prosperity and blessings. And tell them that at the time of their happy deaths the meaning of the messages they delivered will be revealed to them.'"

Nonna took a sip from her cup and wiped her lips with her paper napkin.

"God the Father then said to the archangels, 'And because you obeyed My command and kept these holy secrets, I shall reward you by making you My Son's special friends.'

"The archangels again obeyed God. They visited the Wise Men in their dreams and delivered the promises God had made for them. Of course, the Wise Men did not understand what they were told, but out of obedience each wrote his secret on parchment paper and entrusted his letter to a reliable servant for delivery to each other.

"The messenger sent by one of the Wise Men was a deceitful servant. When he had all the secrets together, he went to Herod and tried to sell them to him. But when Herod heard the messages, he laughed. They made no sense, so he threw the deceitful messenger out of the palace.

"But now the secrets were out. Lucifer now knew the messages, and that put Jesus in great danger. In anger God punished the distrustful servant who had revealed the secret letters. He had to spend the rest of his life never being trusted by anyone.

"Once again God called the archangels and told them that in order to remain friends of Jesus, they would have to face Lucifer, who would now try to stop Jesus from completing His mission.

"So you see, Vincenzo, all secrets are important, even when we think they are unimportant. When a secret is broken, everything turns bad and many people get hurt, even God."

"You heard what happened?" I asked with my head down, totally ashamed to look at her because of what I had done.

"Yes. Your angry friend did not speak in a whisper, so I had to hear that you broke a secret. This time you did something wrong."

"What do I do now?"

"Ask forgiveness and work to regain your friend's trust," my grandmother replied very calmly.

"Suppose he won't forgive me?"

"That will be your punishment. And if he never trusts you again, that will be your greater punishment."

She got up from the chair and walked to the icebox.

I sat at the table knowing that she was right. After some time I said timidly, "I will go to my friend if you promise to tell me what the secrets were that the Wise Men told Jesus."

Nonna smiled as she returned from the icebox, her arms heavy with the bags of vegetables she would need to make supper.

"This is no time for bargaining. This is a serious thing you did. But I know if I don't tell you, you will drive me insane." She put the vegetables on the porcelain table and extended her hand to me.

"This will be a good bargain."

I smiled back and shook her hand in agreement.

"Well, let's see."

She reached into a bag, took a head of lettuce from it, and began breaking off one leaf at a time.

"Well, you see, God the Father never told Jesus what He was to do when He came to earth. So the Magi's messages told Jesus where He had to go to find out what He was to do with His life on earth.

"Now, Caspar, who was from a desert kingdom, told Jesus to go to the desert. There He would teach the gift of faith for all.

"Melchior, who was from a sea kingdom, told Jesus to go to the sea. There He would teach the gift of hope to all.

"Finally, Balthazar, who was from a mountain kingdom, told Jesus to go to the mountain. There He would teach the gift of love to all.

"So you see, Vinzee, with these messages, Jesus knew where He had to go and what His life was to teach. Of course, He taught us faith, hope, and love."

She gathered all the lettuce she needed and went to the kitchen sink to wash it.

"I don't understand," I said.

"Neither did the Wise Men, but they kept the secrets until it was safe to reveal them."

"But, Nonna ..."

"No! No more. Off you go. See your friend. Look in the Bible and see if you can understand. Think it out."

She busied herself with our family supper. I knew I had to do what she told me to do.

Several weeks later, after much reading and thinking and after asking questions of others, I went to my grandmother armed with what I thought were the meanings of the secrets.

"So, Mister Wise Guy, tell me what you have discovered."

"Jesus went to the desert as a Baby to escape King Herod, and later He also went to the desert to fast. Remember, Lucifer was there, because he tempted Jesus. Lucifer had to know where to find Jesus. Jesus was too strong in faith to be tempted by Satan."

I looked at her. "Am I right?" I asked.

"Very good! You are prepared, and I am anxious to hear the rest, but first let me give the finishing touches to the first secret.

"Caspar died at the moment Satan left Jesus. His soul was carried by his messenger, Gabriel, to the site of temptation. As Gabriel comforted Jesus and fed Him, Caspar worshipped Jesus because it was there revealed to him that the Baby of Bethlehem was God."

Happy because I knew I was on the right track, I continued, "When Jesus went to the River Jordan, He met John, who at first didn't want to baptize Him but did it anyway. Later Jesus met the stormy sea, and it was in the Sea of Galilee that Peter failed to walk on water."

"Very good! My goodness, you really have done some looking up. Is there more?"

"No," I replied, with some disappointment that I might have missed something else.

"Well, you have to realize that Lucifer was there to cause John to doubt and for Peter to lose courage. And it was Lucifer who caused the sea to storm so that he could endanger Jesus and His friends. Though he caused these things, he could not beat God. All these things proved hope in Jesus.

"So on the day that Jesus calmed the sea, Melchior died. His soul was taken up in the sky, and he watched the calming of the sea. This is how dear Melchior realized that this Man born in Bethlehem was King and God of the entire universe. It was Michael and his troops of angels who protected Jesus and the others by keeping the devil busy in combat as Jesus calmed the sea."

She smiled, settled more comfortably in the wooden kitchen chair, and asked, "So that leaves us with one more."

"Jesus went to the mountain to teach the Beatitudes and the Our Father," I said. "And He went to the mountain to die."

My grandmother took a deep breath and let out a sigh.

"Hmmm. Yes. It was Raphael who comforted Jesus in Gethsemane. Our friend Balthazar was not as lucky as the other Wise Men. He returned to Jerusalem when he was very old and saw Jesus for the second time in his life. Only he saw Jesus being crucified. The old man's heart was broken, and he became bitter.

But God is good. Raphael came and comforted our poor Balthazar. He didn't take him to heaven right away. Our good God made Balthazar see Jesus for the third time on the day of the Resurrection. Old Balthazar knew that Jesus, the tiny Babe of swaddling clothes and of the stable, was God and man. They say that after he realized this, Balthazar died. You know, Vinzee, now that I think about it, maybe Balthazar was the most blessed of the Wise Men."

We both sat in silence for a few moments. Nonna finally got up, walked to me, and kissed me on my forehead, which was her favorite place to kiss me.

"You did good. I am happy. Now tell me how are things with you and your friend?"

"We are friends again, but still I don't think he trusts me."

"It will come. It will come," Nonna assured me. She turned to the gas range and stirred the stew that was in the pot. Having completed this small but important task, she returned to her chair and said in a low voice: "One thing more, do you remember, in the story it was said that the Wise Men had to whisper their messages to Jesus?"

I nodded my head.

"Well, think about that, Vincenzo."

She lowered her voice even more—to a whisper—and continued, "When a secret is told in trust, it is given in a whisper. It is something only to be heard by one person. Never let a secret go beyond a whisper. Always remember, it was for secrets that God created the whisper."

Six

Heroes

One thing I loved to do was read and collect comic books. I had a very large collection, which I guarded fanatically. I would read and reread them, or on my lazy days I would just skim through them and look at the pictures. As time passed, the characters in these books became my heroes.

The War continued on, and it took its toll on my family. I began to wonder why my superheroes did not go overseas and defeat the enemy. One day I had the thought that maybe no one had asked them for help, so I sat down and printed a letter to one of my biggest heroes and mailed it off. I asked my hero why he had not flown overseas, defeated the enemy, and ended the War. I was certain he could easily do that and all would be good again. I sat back to wait for a response.

One never came, but I relaxed in the sure conviction that any day soon my hero would spring into action and all would be OK.

Of course nothing happened. The longer the War continued, the more disappointed I became with my special hero and all the other superheroes. Soon I was without heroes.

In angry disappointment, when the next paper drive came to my neighborhood, I gathered all my comic books together, walked to the corner, and deposited them all on the pile.

Nonna saw me do it. She decided to commend me on my caring.

"That was very, very good of you, Vinzee. I don't think anyone today gave as much as you gave," she said with a lot of sympathy in her voice.

"I don't need them anymore, Nonna. I don't believe in heroes anymore."

"Oh, that is not so good. Why did you come to this big decision?"

I began to tell her about my letter and all those months of silence—not hearing of, reading of, or seeing any heroic action or any enemy surrenders.

"Heroes don't always have to be heroes," Nonna said. "Sometimes what they did in the past is all that is needed to make them heroes. Some heroes come into life to do just one heroic act and nothing more. God made it happen that way so that we all can be heroes.

"Each of us has one deed to do in life that is meant only for us to do. Now, people like your heroes have many things to do, and that may be the reason why they can't help us win the War. They are too busy, and maybe we have to be heroes and win this war ourselves. Yes, it may be this is what we have to do."

She walked over to me and hugged me close to her.

"Today, because you gave up your comic books, I think you became a hero to many people."

I always remembered what she said, and after that day I had a thousand heroes.

Seven

$\mathcal{D}$ifferent From the Rest of Us

One cold winter day as I was walking home from school with some of my friends, we saw a mutual friend taking out the trash for one of our neighbors. This neighbor was not particularly well-liked by the neighborhood kids because she always complained about our making too much noise or playing in front of her house or sitting on her steps. In fact, she had complained to several of our parents, and we had been punished for annoying her.

I was somewhat surprised to find my friend helping this unpopular lady but decided to ignore what I had seen. However, several of my friends got very angry and decided he should be excluded from all of our activities.

When I got home, I told Nonna what I had seen and what my friends had decided to do. She looked at me with some confusion.

"Come in the kitchen. I have some time before I have to cook for the family. Let's have a little bit of coffee before you start homework."

Still chilled by the cold weather outside, I jumped at this opportunity for something warm. As I passed the icebox, I opened the door, pulled out the milk, and continued to the kitchen table. After Nonna assembled the other things, we sat to drink hot coffee.

"You know," she said quietly, "when God created the birds, He made them all white. He wanted us humans, who would be living with the birds, to see them as reminders that we must be as pure white and as sinless as they are, and that we had to fly in the heavens to get back to Him. Now, you and I know that birds are the nicest creatures God created, and we both know that birds are also the most humble and the happiest of God's creatures. That's why they always are singing."

"Is that why you always feed the birds, Nonna?" I asked, remembering that every crumb of bread that came off our family table was gathered softly in her hand and carried out into the backyard for the birds.

"Yes. I like being a good friend to birds. St. Francis used to sing with the birds, and they befriended him because of that. But more importantly, Francis loved birds because they helped Jesus all through His life on earth."

I searched my brain trying to remember when I had read or heard that *birds* had helped Jesus. I could not recall anything like this.

"Nonna, when did birds help Jesus?" I asked, knowing that she would certainly have a story.

She took a sip of her coffee, moved her chair closer to the kitchen table, and began her explanation.

"A great saint of the world wrote many stories about what birds did for Jesus. Let me see if I can remember some of them. Oh, yes, I'm beginning to remember one of them."

She wet her lips and smiled.

"Well, one very hot summer day, when Jesus was just a little baby, the heat of the day was bothering Him a great deal, and He was becoming very uncomfortable. A small white bird flew by and, seeing how the heat was bothering the Baby Jesus, decided to do something to help Him. He called all his family together. The small bird told his family the problem he had discovered and suggested something to help make Jesus more comfortable.

"The plan was that they would all fly into the blazing sun and begin to flap their wings. Because there were so many of them, they created shade for the Infant Jesus. And because they flapped their wings so much, they created a breeze that fanned the Christ Child.

"But as they continued to do this, their feathers began to get burned and turn brown. To show how He appreciated what the birds had done, Jesus had the feathers on the birds' chests turn orange in memory of the day they cooled Him in the sun. So today a Robin has a brown body and an orange chest."

She stopped for another sip of her coffee and sat upright in her chair. She looked pleased with herself.

"Another time another bird helped Jesus, but in a far different way. This bird watched the scourging at the pillar, and when he saw the pools of Precious Blood on the floor of the prison, he became very sad. He called his family, and together they went and lay in the Blood. They splashed and soaked themselves in the Blood of Jesus. So in memory of this beautiful act, the Cardinal is all red today.

"Still another time, when the Three Wise Men were following the star to Jesus, they lost the star in the daylight. The sky was bright and blue, and they just could not find the star. They were at a standstill and began to worry that the star might move too far from them and they would never be able to find it again.

"Soon one of the white birds that had been following the caravan saw the problem and called his family and friends together. They flew high in the sky, higher than any other bird had ever flown, until they crashed into the blue sky. They then began to brush themselves against the sky until all the light blue turned to dark blue and the star once again became visible to the Three Wise Men. So the Blue Jay got his reward: Today he is light blue like the daytime sky, white like the clouds, and dark blue like the nighttime sky."

Nonna rose from her chair and walked slowly to the cabinet. She removed the big aluminum pot from the cabinet, went to the kitchen sink, and filled the pot with water. I knew we would be having store-bought macaroni for dinner. She carried the water-filled pot to the gas range and turned on the flame.

"There is one more story; it took place on the night King Herod's armies were chasing the Holy Family into Egypt, which was the same night as the killing of the Holy Innocent Babies. On that night, all the angels in heaven were so busy carrying the souls of the innocent babes into heaven that there was no one to spare to watch over the Holy Family as they fled into Egypt. With no one to protect these holy people, it was certain they would be captured.

"St. Gabriel went to God the Father with this problem. The Father with great concern sent St. Raphael down to earth and told him to see if something could be done. Raphael went to the Lion, the King of the Beasts, and told him he had to help out.

"The Lion looked over his kingdom and saw a funny-looking white bird with a long feathery tail. He immediately ordered this bird and all of his kind to line the road to Egypt, spread open their long feathery tails, and hide the Holy Family from the armies of Herod. He further ordered them to keep watch over the Holy Family until they reached safety. The King of the Beasts then went into prayer and asked God to help make his plan work. God the Father heard the Lion's prayer and answered it.

"Out of appreciation and to commemorate this occasion, God painted eyes on the tails of these birds and told them to keep these eyes on all the birds that would do good things for Jesus. That is why the Peacock has such beautiful feathers and a beautiful tail. The Peacock became the eyes of God, and because of him all the other birds in creation have changed their colors. He has to report to God all that the birds have done to help God on earth.

"Now, you remember I said when God created the birds He created them all white. But, you see, as they began to do things for Him, He rewarded them. Today we have all different colored birds because they have done so many good deeds and have been rewarded."

She walked to the cupboard and took out two boxes of macaroni. Returning she stopped by the table and looked at me. I know I must have looked mesmerized. I waited for more to be said.

"Do you understand what I am saying to you, Vinzee? Do you see the connection of these stories to what your friend did? We are all made alike. What makes us different is the good that we do.

"Your friend did good today. He made himself different from the rest of us. If you ask him, he will tell you he feels different inside, good inside, for being nice to that old lady. This is his reward. He was changed, and this has made him different from the rest of us. Maybe you should tell your other friends about the birds and what they did, and maybe they will not be so unkind."

Eight

𝒯he Bigger They Are, the Louder They Are

I was always asking my grandmother questions. Among the questions were those I liked to call the "how comes." These were usually questions about why things were the way they were. Now when I think of her stories, I realize that maturity and education have wrecked many of the "truths" she told me. But there are times when I find the truths of my youth better than the cold knowledge of maturity.

In the Garden of Gethsemane was a group of animals. These animals had lived in this garden for many years. Most of them were small animals, but there were some larger ones. And these larger animals bullied and bossed the smaller ones around.

The larger animals also took on the duty of defending the garden from other animals. They enforced the law that no new animal was ever permitted to build a home in this garden. Further, any animal entering the garden, even if it was just passing through, was to be met immediately with hostilities from the larger animals and eventually beaten off. This made the small group of animals in the garden very clannish and at times very snobbish.

Now, Jesus and His chosen apostles would often come to

the garden to pray. This made the animals even more snobbish, because they believed that they alone had been chosen
to be with Jesus, the Son of God. No other group of animals
could claim to have been in His company as often as they had
been. When the opportunity was theirs, they often would brag
to other animals of how important they were to the garden
and to Jesus. Most of the bragging came from the larger animals, who would boast to passers-by. They often said that their
purpose in life was to watch over and protect Jesus and His
twelve friends.

But in truth, when Jesus came to the garden, only the smaller animals would sit and silently watch Him as if to guard Him.
The larger animals would go about being braggarts and bullies.

One night Jesus and His twelve apostles came into the garden. All the animals somehow sensed this was not to be an
ordinary night. When the apostles did not stay with Jesus, but
instead went off to the side and fell fast asleep, the animals
knew something was very wrong. The Mouse, who had been
with Jesus earlier that night, reported that the apostles were
fast asleep because they had been drinking wine.

The animals noticed that Jesus seemed very somber, more
than usual. They heard Jesus speak, and from His voice they
realized that He was very troubled. Out of sheer concern, all
the animals in the garden stood watch that night. As the hour
moved on, some of them even began to cry silently for Jesus.

They became doubly saddened when He went to the apostles
and asked them to join Him. When His followers continued to
sleep, the animals in silence drew closer to Jesus to keep Him
company and to watch over Him. They didn't want to leave
Him alone. They watched in awe as bloody sweat came to His

brow. Some wanted to go to Him, but the larger animals ordered them to remain still.

When the angel came to comfort Jesus, the animals all sighed with relief. But their sighs gave them away, and Jesus looked over His shoulder in their direction. He smiled warmly. It was the only time He smiled that night, and the last time He would ever smile.

Suddenly one of the small birds arrived. His excited chirping broke the silence of the garden.

"Many angry men are coming toward the garden," he said. "They are carrying torches, clubs, and spears."

The smaller animals grew frightened.

"What are they coming here for?" the big brave Reindeer buck asked.

"They are coming to get Jesus and hurt Him," the small Bird replied.

"No! Never will this happen," the big wise Owl said. "We must not let this happen. We cannot let it happen."

Immediately the bigger animals took defensive positions and vowed they would protect Jesus from harm. They would use their big horns, their loud roars, their long claws, and their sharp teeth. The smaller animals, not to be outdone, vowed to help also.

In the distance they heard the sound of the crowd. The animals all grew silent and continued to watch Jesus. His sadness hurt them all. In minutes they began to see that He was regaining His strength. No doubt they thought this was because He knew the animals were near and ready to protect Him.

The sounds of humans grew louder, and the light from their torches brighter. It was a big crowd.

"Do you think we will be able to defend Jesus?" asked the big silvery Fox nervously.

No one answered him. They all seemed too preoccupied with their own fears. The sound of the mob was much louder, and the sound of their feet much closer.

"They probably have real sharp sticks, swords, and spears," stated the big white Wolf anxiously.

No one answered him, because now they were all terrified. Jesus stood up from His rock. His face, shining in the full moon, was silvery and sad.

"If He calls His apostles, they will defend Him," stated the small gray Squirrel. His voice trembled slightly.

"Why don't they wake up?" asked the Raccoon.

Now the mob was closer and louder.

"My God," exclaimed the Possum, swinging from a tree branch. "There are thousands of them, and they are all armed. We will not be able to defend Jesus."

The animals saw the apostles stir from their sleep.

"Look, the others are getting up," said the Coyote excitedly.

"They will defend Jesus better than we small creatures can," hissed the black Garden Snake.

"You are right! We better leave it all to them," squalled the Raven, and with that the animals scampered off, all running in different directions. Many shivered with fear and were unable to run their fastest, but others found their full potential immediately.

They all left except one small furry black animal. This animal, though filled with the same fear as the others, vowed aloud that he would stay to defend Jesus. And with that statement he ran from the shadows of the garden bushes and stood before Jesus, prepared to defend Him from the mob.

"Stand firm," the small animal said to Jesus. "Just stand behind me. I'll scare this mad gang off. Just stand firm, behind me."

Jesus looked down and said, "My dear friend, though I know you will defend Me with your life, it will not help. For what is taking place here is the will of our Father, your God. Go, let Me do what is required of Me, for what was required of you, you have done and done well."

The little animal turned to face Jesus. He stood on his hind legs. His big dark eyes sparkled with tears. He wanted so much to do more.

"I shall remember you and your kind forever. Now you must go!"

With that the animal obediently ran away. As he passed Jesus, his back touched the hem of His robe. And that is why even to this day the Skunk has a white stripe down his back.

Nine

*A*lways Leave a Little Undone

There was a boy in our neighborhood whom no one seemed to like. One summer day, for reasons I cannot remember, several of my friends began picking on this boy. I came on the scene late and was witness to some cruel verbal abuse. The boy who was disliked just stood in silence. I saw the tears welling in his eyes out of hurt or frustration or anger. He could do nothing. He was outnumbered and fragile in comparison to his abusers.

After my friends had finished their unkindness and it was safe, I walked over to the boy and helped pick up his belongings, which had been thrown about by my friends. Much to my surprise, I apologized for what my friends had done to him.

Many months later this boy died of a fatal illness that none of us knew he had. All my friends mourned his death as if he had been the best friend they ever had. This hypocrisy drove a wedge into my friendship with some of them. I was more of a friend to this boy than they were. Yet I went to his viewing regretting that I had not done much more to help him or befriend him. Months after this boy's death I spoke to Nonna about my feelings.

"Evil multiplies itself quickly," she said, "but kindness multiplies even faster and is long remembered." She pinched my cheek. "I am proud of you. You did what you thought was right."

She examined my face and saw that her praise had not settled my self-punishment. She smiled. Walking to the gas range she said, "A great and well-known bishop from my province in Italy wrote a story about saints who thought they had to do more. Come, sit and we shall talk."

She took my hand gently and led me to the kitchen table.

"Well, this story goes back many years—oh, I'd say to the time right after the Crucifixion. Now, the apostles were afraid of the authorities and the leaders of the people. They never went out during the daytime, because they were afraid of being recognized. They would go out only under the cover of night."

She sat back in her chair, crossed her ankles, and folded her arms across her breast. There was satisfaction in her voice as she continued.

"But the women followers of Jesus were not afraid, and they went out day and night. Among the women was, of course, Mary, the Mother of Jesus. So on the Fridays after Good Friday the Blessed Mother would slip out of the house with Mary Magdalene, Joanna, Salome, and the other Mary. The small group of ladies walked across the city through the very narrow streets that Jesus had walked on His way to Calvary. This made them feel close to Him, and they remembered. You see, they wanted to remember the day of His death.

"Every Friday thereafter, long after Pentecost and long after the apostles left for distant lands, Mary and the other women would devoutly walk this way of sorrows. As you know, this was the beginning of the Stations of the Cross. Did you know that our great St. Francis of Assisi took this custom back to Italy when he returned from Jerusalem?"

I smiled and nodded, knowing this fact because she had told me so many times over and over.

"Now, after walking this way for a few weeks, Magdalene began to notice something very peculiar: Every time they came to this one particular place on their Way of the Cross, she saw a tall muscular black man standing silently against the wall. He always looked as if he were in prayer, and his face was always very sad.

"One week Magdalene noticed that this same black man had been joined by another black man, who was much older and had pure white hair and a white beard. Magdalene mentioned her observation to the other women, including the Blessed Mother.

"When told of Magdalene's discovery, the Blessed Mary said, 'I also noticed these men, and one of them reminds me of someone I knew. The next time we go to pray "The Way," we will stop and talk to them.'

"'But, Mary, do you really think this wise? They are perfect strangers. God alone knows what they are doing there,' said Joanna.

"'Whatever their doings, we shall find out,' Mary replied gently.

"So the next Friday the ladies once again went out to walk the streets of Jerusalem along 'The Way.' When they came to the two black strangers, Mary walked directly to them, followed somewhat timidly by the other holy ladies.

"'Kind sirs, please help me,' Mary started. 'I and my companions have been coming this way for many Fridays and could not help but notice each time we come by that you are here.'

"'We are just remembering a friend,' the younger man stated, as the older man nodded in agreement.

"'May I ask who this someone is?' Mary inquired.

"'It was the Nazarene, Jesus,' the young man answered quickly but with sadness in his voice.

"Mary was somewhat confused. She knew all of Jesus' companions, but never had she seen these men among them.

"'How did you come to know Jesus?' Mary asked with curiosity.

"'I never met Him till the day of His death,' said the younger man, 'but I feel I have known Him forever. I know that what He was doing that day was something far greater than what anyone saw. He was doing something more powerful than just dying.

"'Look at me, Madam. Do I look like a man who would find carrying a cross difficult? Yet when they pressed me into service to help Him carry His Cross, I succumbed to weakness, and I could not do more for Him.' His eyes began to fill with tears. 'And when He looked into my eyes, when He looked ... He read me.... He read all of me and left me His servant forever.'

"'He could read us all,' said the old man quietly. 'I have known this Jesus for many years. He once looked at me also, and without speaking a word, my life was His.

"'I was away from Jerusalem for years and recently returned to find Him. I arrived the day of His triumph, and I needed to see no more, for He was the King I always knew He would be. Satisfied with what I saw, I planned to return home within a week.

"'But when I heard that He was to be killed, I cursed the day I came back. I watched in horror the death walk through these narrow streets. I prayed for the strength of my youth to return to me so I could help Him, but old and frail I could do nothing. When I saw His beaten face and swollen lips, I ran to a nearby well, scooped up a cup of water, and ran through the crowds to His side. But a soldier threw me to the ground. I was too old, too weak, to get up to do more.

"'Then I cried to God, "Blind me! Let me see no more." My prayers were answered. I now will see no more, except the beaten face of the King.'"

Mary sighed softly with pity and sorrow.

"'But Madam, I have great sight now, for I understand many things.' The old man's voice dropped to a whisper. 'At the moment of my blindness, I saw that this Jesus was the Son of God. My blindness has been a great blessing, for the last thing I saw was the Face of God.'

"'And I, when I was carrying His cross, learned a similar thing,' said the young man. 'I learned that this Man, Jesus, was carrying the weight of the world in that cross, and no man but One who was God could have done that.'

"Mary and the ladies stood in awe of these two men, now both with tears falling from their faces. Mary wanted to reach out and hold them. These were truly Jesus' friends.

"'Please, sirs, tell me your names, so that I may remember you in my prayers of gratitude.'

"'I am called Simon Ben Africanus of Cyrene,' said the young man.

"'Oh, Simon,' Mary said, her voice filled with joy. 'You did all that could have been done for Jesus. You did more than most will ever do for Him. I am sure that Jesus remembers you above all others, for you partook of His pains. You lived them with Him. When all had left Him, you were there. I know what you have done has pleased my Son Jesus.'

"'"My Son"! Jesus is your Son? Oh! Oh, my Lady!' the older man said as he struggled and staggered to his feet to bow to Mary. 'My Lady, it has been years. I am Balthazar, the Magus from Cyrene.'

"'Oh, sweet friend,' Mary said, her eyes filling with tears of joy. 'I thought your face was familiar. God has been good to let me see you once again. How blessed we both have been, for we have known Jesus as a Child and then as a Man. How could you feel you had not done enough for Jesus? How could you feel you had failed Him? You should never feel so. You sought him twice, and each time you saw Him as a King. Please be happy, for you have been blessed twofold.'

"Turning to the ladies near her she said, 'This is a time of rejoicing, my daughters. Come, Simon and Balthazar, friends, come and eat with us.'

"Again turning to her companions, she said, 'Ladies, please go and prepare a meal for Jesus' dearest friends.'"

My grandmother's voice had now became a whisper, "Balthazar stayed with Mary until he died in her arms, the same arms that had held the Baby Jesus. Simon returned to Cyrene, where years later he was crucified for being a follower of Jesus. These men were not expected to be braver or stronger on Good Friday. They were expected to do the little they did, for this was all that was expected of them and all they could do, and Jesus did the rest. So it is with you."

She got up from her chair and returned to her cleaning. I

sat a few moments. There was more to this story, but it would come later. For those moments I reflected on this being a good story of friendship, and I remember thinking that Jesus had a lot of different friends: old and young; strong and weak; white and black.

I didn't know if this was what Nonna wanted me to know, but this is what I was thinking when I heard her say, "We are always expected to do what is needed in the time given us. God knows and keeps the other times for Himself. If we did everything, who would need God? If God did everything, who would need us? If at the time we can do no more, then it is always wise to leave just a little undone."

Ten

$\mathcal{N}$onna, Jesus Is at the Door

Nonna was in the kitchen. She was just about to begin supper. I knew this because I could hear the pots and pans clanking and banging, and I could hear her humming the tune to one of the folk songs from her home province in Italy. I knew soon she would begin singing because this was her pattern: She always sang after she hummed for a while, and her singing would add to the beauty of the moment. Nonna would sing a lot if it were a holiday or a birthday or if she was doing something special for someone else.

All my cousins were out of the house playing and doing other things, so I had the house with all its comforts and all its rare peace to myself. I selfishly dreaded the idea of the family's coming home and breaking into my tranquility. It was a very cold winter day, and I was sitting on the couch under my coat, enjoying the warmth of our centralized coal heater. I was reading about the feudal system from my history book. Sr. Mary Eulalia had instructed us to know all about this chapter for a big test. I loved history, so reading this chapter and studying it was a joy.

Nonna began to sing. I lowered my book and joyfully listened to her soft, nice-sounding voice. The song she was singing was very familiar to me, so I began to quietly sing along.

It was a typical Italian song of love and suffering. It told of the silent love a young farm boy had for a girl whose father owned the farm he worked. She was, of course, of higher economic, educational, and social standing. The girl became ill and was near death. She told the boy's mother, who worked as a servant in the girl's house, that if she died she would not die happy for she had never found love: She was never loved by anyone besides her parents. The mother told the young boy, and at night he sneaked into her bedroom. As she lay in a deep sleep, he told her of his deep love for her. She died in his arms happy, for there was someone other than her parents who loved her.

After the song was over, the house returned to silence. I thought to myself how lucky I was, having been born into my family. I was so blessed to live with them and to love them and for them to love me. I took a deep breath, proud to have been so greatly blessed.

Your world is the greatest, I thought to myself. *There is nothing in God's world that could possibly bother you.* I shifted my body on the couch, wanting to get more comfortable as I returned to the land of serfs, lords, and castles.

Abruptly there was a knock on the door. It wasn't a rough or demanding knock, but it broke the moment and it sounded like a bomb. I ignored it, hoping and praying it would go away, but the bomb came again.

"Vinzee," I heard Nonna call from the kitchen, "answer the door."

"All right," I said as I got off the couch and walked to the front door. I began mumbling and grumbling under my breath: *This better be important,* I thought. *If it isn't, I will hate whoever bothered me.* I was certain that it was one of my cousins.

I opened the door, and there on the bottom step was a haggard-looking man with a three- or four-day-old beard wearing tattered clothes and a bedraggled hat that was pulled over his ears. His arms were folded across the thin suit jacket he was wearing, as he tried to keep whatever body warmth he had to himself. He shifted and bobbed on his feet, hoping to keep the blood flowing in his body. Immediately, as a defense, I partially closed the door. My friends would have called this man a bum or a hobo or a tramp. All three names struck fear and disgust in our hearts.

"I'm sorry to bother you," he said with quivering lips. "But do you have any change to spare so I can get something to eat?"

"No," I said roughly. But I quickly took the edge off my voice, "I don't have any money."

I felt sorry for the man, but I wasn't telling a lie. I had no money on me.

"Sorry to bother you," he said as he quickly turned and walked away from the steps.

I closed the door and dashed back to my warm couch and coat.

"Who was that at the door?" Nonna asked.

"Oh, no one important. It was a bum," I called back to her.

There was a long heavy silence, and I knew I had made a mistake.

"Nonna?"

"What did the man want?" she called back.

"Money. I told him I didn't have any, and he went away."

There was a heavy silence again. I heard her soft steps coming from the kitchen through the dinette, through the dining room, and into the living room. She walked directly to the front door, which she quickly opened. I knew she was looking for the man, and I knew what was coming next. So I got up, put on my shoes, and was already reaching for my coat when she shut the door and walked back into the living room.

"Put on your shoes and coat," she commanded, "and go find that man and bring him back here. Hurry before it is too late."

"I wasn't lying, Nonna," I said in defense of myself as I threw on my coat. "I didn't have any money on me."

"Neither do I, but did he look hungry? Do you think we could give him something to eat? Hurry. Go find him!"

I ran out of the house. The cold winter air smacked me in the face unkindly. I looked quickly up the street and saw the man walking down to the corner of our block. When I caught up to him, I timidly reached for his shoulder and tapped him. He swung around, startled and surprised.

"We don't have any money, Mister, but my grandmother said she could give you something to eat."

"Oh, that will be great. That's what I need."

"Follow me," I said. I turned and began to walk very rapidly toward our house.

I didn't want any of my friends to see me with this guy, so I made certain that I kept him well behind me. Finally we reached our house. I quickly ran up the steps and into the house, closing the door behind me.

"Nonna, that man is here. He is at the door," I shouted as I walked through the house to the kitchen.

"Good, now go tell him to wait. Then come back and help me make a sandwich."

I did as she said. When I returned to the kitchen, she had

the sliced bread and the jars of peanut butter and jelly on the table.

"Hurry, make the sandwich. I have put some water on for a cup of tea," she said as she rummaged through the cabinet looking for something.

I made the sandwich, really packing it with peanut butter and jelly.

"Here, wrap it up in some wax paper and put it in a brown paper bag. And here, give him some of my homemade cookies," she said as she turned from the gas range with one of our old cups brimming with hot tea.

"Now, let's go," she said. I walked in front, and she followed slowly so as not to spill any of the tea. When we arrived at the front door, the man was sitting on the step curled up trying to keep warm. He looked up, and his face beamed his joy and relief.

"Vinzee, you talk so that he will not misunderstand me," Nonna said in Italian.

"Tell him we give him a sandwich, some cookies, and tea and that he can keep the cup."

After I told the man in English what Nonna had said, she told me to go into the dining room clothes closet and get my old scarf for the man. I did as I was told, finding that it felt good to be doing all these nice things for this man.

"Thank you, lady. You have given me another day to live," the man said, as he quickly walked away.

"What did he say, Vinzee?"

I repeated in Italian what he had said, and she stood upright, smiled, and closed the door.

I quickly ran to the couch, curled up, and returned to the moats and drawbridges and manors of the feudal system. I sensed Nonna lingering nearby, and I knew I was about to be reprimanded for calling that man a bum.

"We have a lesson here, Vincenzo. Never call someone a bum. Only God knows why that man is the way he is. But no matter how he got that way, he still was cold and hungry."

I cautiously glanced over the top of my history book, realizing this was not to be a major reprimand.

Nonna continued, "Maybe it was a blessing that we had no money to give him, because giving him money could have made him hurt himself further. But always remember there is something you can do or give—if not money then food, water, or some other kindness.

"Remember, you never know who is behind a knock on the door. Do you remember what Jesus said, 'When I was hungry, you fed Me, and when I was thirsty, you gave Me to drink, and when I was cold, you clothed Me'? Well, that man could have been Jesus or one of His messengers coming to give us a test or an opportunity to do a good deed. If we had sent him away hungry and cold, we would have turned away Jesus and lost a chance to return love."

She turned and walked into the kitchen. When my cousins came in later, I told them what had happened. From that time on anyone who came to our door was greeted kindly and given what could be given.

As time went on, when any of my cousins or I answered the door and there was a stranger there, we would call to our grandmother in Italian, "Nonna, Jesus is at the door."

Eleven

You Don't Need a Bolt of Lightning

I always prided myself on being a perfect altar boy. One day a classmate of mine said that he thought I was not serving the funeral Masses correctly. He told me he had heard Father remark that I was not holding the thurible properly. Of course, I balked at his remarks and told him I didn't believe that Father had said this or that he knew what he was talking about.

I sulked for days. I was hurt and offended that I had been thought imperfect in my service to God. After several days of this self-pity, I approached my grandmother and told her what the boy had said.

"So, you don't believe your friend, and you don't believe what he said Father said? Well ... there is always some truth in what people say. You should listen to your friend."

"Why, he could be fibbing."

"Why would he? If you cannot find an answer to that question, you must listen to your friend."

"I think he is jealous of me."

Nonna continued with her cleaning duties. Suddenly she stopped, looked at me, and smiled.

"You remind me of Fiato."

"Who?" I questioned with wonderment.

"Fiato. He was the main character in a story by one of Italy's greatest writers. Fiato was a rooster. He believed he was a very good rooster, and he was extremely proud of being a very good rooster. It was his duty to give the midnight crow to the soldiers of the Roman Army. Well, one day while he was sleeping, word got around the chicken house (that was the place where Fiato and the other roosters lived) that on that particular night the animals were to be quiet and suspend all of their normal activities. There was much sadness in the air all day long. That night was a very cold night, and most of the animals said it seemed to be the darkest night of all nights."

She stopped cleaning.

"Would you like some coffee? Good."

She led the way to the kitchen, retrieved the milk and, because of the War rations, the brown sugar, and poured the coffee. She sat down, letting out a sigh of relief. Carefully she lifted the cup to her lips, took a sip of coffee, and continued.

"Finally Fiato got up from his sleep. It was near midnight. He gargled and spruced up his big-feathered chest. He pranced proudly before the mirror and then began his breathing exercises.

"Just then one of the younger roosters, a friend of his called Saggio, came walking by and said, 'Tonight is a foul night. There is something wrong in the air. Don't you feel it? We all feel it. I would suggest you not crow tonight.'

"'You don't know what you are talking about. It's like any other night, just a bit colder.'

"'No. I tell you, tonight is different,' Saggio said. 'We got word to be very careful in all we do and say tonight.'

"'And who gave you this word?' Fiato clucked back.

"'We heard it from the old Rooster, who got it from the Owl, who got the word from the King of the Beasts.'

"'And you believe this? All these fools telling each other? Stop being an old hen. I will do what I'm supposed to do.'

"With that Fiato pranced out of the chicken house. *They're just jealous of me because I'm the best rooster,* he thought to himself proudly.

"The night air caught his breath. It was a cold night, and it was the darkest night he had ever seen.

"*Ah, it is only natural during this time of year,* he thought.

"He continued to walk to the highest wall overlooking the city. He took a deep breath, extended his neck, opened his beak, and crowed. His voice cut through the cold night air and sounded louder and richer than ever before. It seemed to travel for miles. He was very pleased yet bewildered by the clarity of his crow, because he had never sounded so strong. He looked over the city. It was dark except for a few large fires the soldiers were burning to keep warm. Again he took a deep breath, extended his neck, and crowed. His voice pierced the dense stillness of the night, and it seemed to echo back to him. Again he was a little startled by the strength of his crow but pleased with himself.

"*This is a good night,* he thought. *What do those jealous fools know about my great crowing?*

"He glanced over the countryside and became aware of the silence of the night. Something *was* wrong. What could it be? The countryside was empty. No humans were moving. It was a strange and very, very quiet night. His friend was right, it was a foul night.

"Again he prepared to crow, a little uneasy but still proud of himself. He took a deep breath. His voice sliced the darkness and sounded the loudest he ever had heard it.

"It's the wind, he thought. *It is carrying my crows further.* Yet once again he thought, *Something is wrong tonight. Maybe I should have listened to my young friend.*

"Suddenly he knew what was wrong. It was the animals! There were no animals out. No owls hooting. No lions hunting. They were all in hiding. They all knew something.

"Just then he saw the figure of a man running aimlessly on the hillside. He was shouting something. It sounded as if he was cursing something or someone. Fiato tried to make out what he was shouting, and after a few moments of straining he heard the man say: 'I have done a bad and evil thing. I am doomed! I must hide. I must run. I must get out of here!'

"The man continued to run and several times stumbled and fell. Finally he was gone—swallowed up by the cold, the darkness, and the night.

"Fiato was confused. He was about to return to the chicken house when, off in the distance, he saw another man come running from the city gates. This man also was running aimlessly, blindly. He was banging and bumping into things. His pace was much faster than the first man's. Fiato stayed on the wall. These goings-on were very unusual, even for crazy humans. He was mesmerized.

"The second man now was running faster and in his direction. Finally he reached Fiato, and he stumbled and fell not too far from Fiato's wall. His face was dark, and Fiato could see the tears that were streaming from his eyes. The moon reflected off the tears, and they looked like shimmering streams of silver rolling down his grim face.

"The man fell like a heap of used rags before the wall. He was sobbing bitterly, and his cries were deep and painful. He looked up and saw Fiato.

"'Oh, Rooster,' he stammered. 'Tonight ... you should not have crowed ... for the sake of my soul.... I have denied my Lord ... I have denied the very purpose of life. Forgive me ... forgive me, Lord!'

"The man rose to his feet and ran off, falling against trees and bushes. He screamed back as he ran, 'Crow no more. Please. Crow no more.'

"Fiato stayed on the wall paralyzed with shock. He had done this? Whatever it was! He had become a part of something never done before. He was a party to a bad thing. Just then an unexpected wind passed by him. It pushed him, and he lost his balance and fell into the yard below without a sound."

My grandmother looked at me for a long time.

"You hear a lesson in this story, Vincenzo?"

"Yes, Nonna, I do. Do you think I should see Father tomorrow?"

"Yes, and listen to him."

She got up quickly from her chair and walked to the kitchen sink to wash her cup.

"Nonna, whatever happened to Fiato? Did he ever crow again?"

"No. Never. You see, he had not trusted others. He became a part of something wrong, and so he repented by giving up what he thought he did best. In the animal kingdom he is always remembered as the only animal mentioned in the Passion of Jesus. Because of his mistake and because he repented, the other roosters built a monument to him."

"Where is his monument?" I asked, smiling a bit because I was sure there could never be a monument to a stupid rooster named Fiato.

"The next time you pass by a farm, look at the roof of the barn. There is Fiato."

She smiled sadly.

I didn't need a bolt of lightning.

Twelve

$\mathcal{U}$gly Hides Beauty and Truth

One day my grandmother caught me in a lie. More than the lie, it was being caught that bothered me the most. It put me in a foul mood. Catching me in a lie really bothered my grandmother, but she did not say a word to me about it. Later that same day I mentioned to my cousin Mary Jane how ugly someone was and how I refused to be bothered with that person.

When Nonna overheard my ugly remark, I heard her let out a loud sigh. It was, I was sure, her last breath of patience. She called me to her side.

"Sit down, Signore." She pointed to the chair by the kitchen table. "I have to talk to you."

There was a tone to her voice that left no doubt about her displeasure, and the fact that she used the word *"Signore,"* which she used only when she was furious with me, further convinced me I was in trouble. My only defense would be to listen to her and receive my punishment.

"They say that people who talk ugly about other people are themselves ugly." She spoke without looking at me. "Here inside," she pointed to her heart. "So don't ever talk ugly unless you first see the ugly in yourself."

She cleared her throat, raised her eyes, and looked at me for a long time. Normally, when she would give me one of these long looks, I would hold my ground and stare back in defiance, but this long, long look aroused no defiance. I began to feel sorry for myself. This was going to be a rough talk.

"They also say that people who lie are cowards and have lost the virtue of honesty even in themselves. So when you lie again, look and see how honest you are with yourself. If you cannot be honest with yourself, you have died a little up here." She pointed to her head.

She turned quickly and walked to the breadbox and took out a loaf of hard-crusted Italian bread. Returning to the kitchen table, she placed the bread on it and walked to the icebox. She removed some Italian cold cuts and some fried hot peppers, returned to the table, and deposited them on it. I now knew she was angry, because she was feeding me and not just offering me coffee. I was about to get the double whammie.

"There was a story written many years ago by a great man. They say this story is one of the truest stories ever told about Jesus. It tells of the time after Jesus died.

"The Jewish people have a very beautiful custom for mourning their dead. I don't remember the Jewish word for it, but the family is to sit in silence without distractions. A lot of my Jewish friends have told me that during this time the memory of the dead person is deeply impressed on their hearts and in their minds. It is also during this time that people come to the deceased's family and tell them all the good things they know about the dead person. It is good for the family to hear these things. It helps ease their pain.

"Well, anyway, when Jesus died, Mary, His Mother, followed this beautiful custom. The other holy women—Mary Magdalene,

Joanna, Salome, and Mary the wife of Cleophus—stayed with her. Now, on the Saturday immediately after Good Friday, Mary and the holy women quietly slipped out of the house, where the apostles were hiding, and went to the tomb where Jesus lay. It was not yet dark, but it was late in the day, maybe just before sunset."

My grandmother paused and began making sandwiches for us. Sandwich-making was an art to her. She was able to pack a large amount of Italian cold cuts between two slices of Italian bread with such ease and exactness. This was because she made her sandwiches with love as the major ingredient.

Having finished making my sandwich, she placed it before me on a dish. Next to the sandwich rested an ugly, wrinkled, distorted, fried, red hot pepper. She sat in her chair and took a small bite from her sandwich.

"Finally they came to the place where Jesus was buried. Exhausted, they quietly sat on the rocks nearby. The hired guards were still there, but they had grown a little tired of their stupid duty and were totally bored. They walked about aimlessly, talking among themselves, and were not really watching the tomb. When they saw the group of ladies come into the area, they called out a warning. Magdalene responded by telling them that the Mother of the dead Man was among them and wanted to visit the tomb. The guards turned back to their private conversations.

"Mary, Jesus' Mother, sat in silence. Her body began to sway slowly back and forth as her mind, her memories, went back through the years. Her heart grew heavy, but she did not find herself feeling sorrow for her own loss. Mankind had killed the one true God, and this sin troubled and frightened her.

She placed herself before God and prayed for all who had been a part of this great crime.

"Suddenly she felt a small stir in the group and heard some low gasps. She opened her eyes, and there before her was a Roman soldier. His face was badly scarred. His nose was crooked, apparently from being broken several times. His cheeks were scarred, and his lower lip twisted and partly missing, most likely from combat. One of his eyes was partly sealed shut, no doubt also from combat, and one of his ears was badly disfigured. When he smiled, it was apparent that several of his teeth were missing and several were broken. He was not easy to look at.

"The other women drew back in disgust, and some of them covered their eyes.

"'Woman,' he said, his good eye examining Mary's face. 'Are you not the Mother of Him who lies here?'

"Mary's heart began to beat rapidly. Images of Calvary returned to her mind and sent a shiver through her body. She drew her cloak to her mouth as if to muffle a cry. She closed her eyes again, hoping to shut the scene from her mind. When it was gone, she looked at the guard. She knew who he was, and for a quick moment his ugliness fit his crime.

"Mary quickly regained her composure and said, 'Yes, I am Mary, the Mother of Jesus.'

"'You know who I am, do you not?'

"'Yes, I know you.'

"'I follow orders, Mother. I am but a tool, an instrument of the authorities. I have no personal reasons....'

"'I know this. I also know that we are all tools and instruments of authority. The difference lies in which authority, man's or God's. If we are of man's authority, then we can do

ugly and evil things as well as good. If we are of God's authority, then we can do only beauty and good. Being of God helps
us see things differently.'

"'I do not know much of your God. I only know what I feel.'

"'And what did you feel yesterday?'

"'I felt I was helping Jesus, just as my friend Abenadar, the
Syrian, did when he forced that man to help carry the cross. If
I had followed the normal ways, Jesus might have suffered
more.'

"Mary now looked at the soldier in a different way, for she
saw remorse in his eye.

"'Tell me,' she asked, 'what do you feel now?'

"'I feel Jesus has helped me, just as He helped my friend,
Cornelius, the centurion. Since Jesus' death, Cornelius is a
changed man. He told me he is at peace with his life, that the
world has changed for him. When the storms came yesterday,
Cornelius said he knew truly who Jesus was. I believe him, for
in all the turmoil on the Mount that day, I heard him cry out,
"Truly, this is the Son of God."'

"'And you, what do you say?'

"'Look at me, Madam,' he said, pointing to his scarred eye.
'Before yesterday I could not see out of this eye, and the other
eye was constantly twitching. Today I have sight in this eye, and
the other has stopped twitching. I can truly see! A miracle
took place in my life, and I know it is because of Jesus.'

"Suddenly, as if by divine revelation, Magdalene said, 'I
know you! You are the one who pierced the side of Jesus.'

"'Yes, I am Longinus.' He lowered his head. 'Few saw what
happened at that moment. As I thrust my spear into His side,
His blood squirted out and splashed against my eyes—and I

was healed!' He raised his head, and his face glowed with joy. He looked at the guards around him, then turned to the women and said in a soft whisper, 'I heard it said that Jesus performed many miracles. Is this true?'

"'Yes,' Mary said softly.

"'Good Lady, with your permission I would like you to meet my two other friends, Abenadar and Cornelius. I shall be off duty soon, and I would like to bring them to you. The three of us have wanted to find and talk to some of His followers. We want to—no, we need to—know more about Him. Please. Give us your permission.'

"'Mary, be careful,' Mary the wife of Cleophus said firmly.

"The Blessed Mother sat silently for a few moments, then finally said, 'The time will come, my friend, when you will meet all the followers of Jesus. Be patient. I suggest you and your companions pray and wait for God's will to be done. We cannot rush the needs of God. They come when we least expect them and when God wills.'

"'Thank you, My Lady.' Longinus bowed, his face beaming with joy and a smile. 'We will wait for God's time.'

"He looked at the others. 'Ladies, I am also your servant.'

"He turned and within seconds was gone from sight. The ladies returned to their silence. They all pondered their own thoughts and their own memories. Mary smiled at the continuing wonders and works of her Son. Magdalene thanked God in silence, for she understood the miracle of Longinus. Salome, Joanna, and the other Mary still reeled from seeing the grotesque features of Longinus but also from witnessing the wonder of God's love.

"But soon their thoughts were again interrupted, this time

by sobs. Sobs so loud as to come from the very soul of the person crying. The group looked around. Much to their surprise they saw a small, fragile young woman sitting on a rock nearby. She was alone. Her dress was modest and simple. She wore a sheer veil over her head. Over her left arm she carried an expensive cloak. The whiteness of the cloak was blinding. She held it close to herself, her right hand resting on it, as if to protect it. She continued to sob, and her sobs were tormenting.

"Mary asked Salome to go ask the girl to join them. At first the young woman would not come, but when Salome told her that she and the others were friends of Jesus, the girl slowly and timidly walked over to them. Immediately Mother Mary reached out and took her in her arms.

"'My dear child, what is causing so many tears and so deep a sorrow? You are far too beautiful and too young to be in such a state.'

"'I am so alone!' the young woman cried. 'I am without a home. My father has disowned me because I refused to marry the one he chose for me.'

"'And why do you not want to marry?' the wife of Cleophus asked.

"'Some time ago I was very sick, near death. My mother, now dead, quietly took me to see Jesus. He cured me, and I promised my mother that I would not marry when I was older. I vowed to remain faithful to Jesus and follow Him forever. Whenever Jesus came to Jerusalem, I would seek Him out in secret and follow Him for days. I found so much joy and peace and love in His words. My father refused to believe my cure or to honor my promise, and he demanded that I not see Jesus again.

"'Several weeks ago he purchased a marriage veil for me. It

was not the most expensive. It was wool but seamless. I reminded him of my promise to my mother, and he told me that if I did not marry, he would disown me and throw me out of his house.

"'On the day that Jesus was crucified, I was in my father's house doing my household duties. I had not heard anything of His arrest or of His sentencing. I had finished all my work, and out of curiosity I decided to try on my bridal shawl.

"'Just then I heard crowds outside. I ran to the door and saw the procession approaching my father's house. I hate crucifixions and decided immediately to lock the door and stay inside. I then heard someone say it was Jesus. I went out and pushed my way through the crowd, with anguish in my heart.

"'There was a man carrying his cross, struggling and staggering along. His face was so badly beaten and bloody that I could not tell who he was. A soldier pushed me back, but I made my way to the oncoming condemned man. I still could not be sure, so I removed my bridal veil from my head and wiped His face. Oh, God of Israel! It was Jesus!'

"Some of the other women began to cry. The girl began to sob loudly again, and Mother Mary reached out to hold her more closely. Slowly the girl began to regain her composure, and then she continued her story."

Again my grandmother paused. She took another bite of her sandwich, and I quickly imitated her. After swallowing her bite, she wiped her mouth with a paper napkin.

"'The soldiers had pushed me to the cobblestoned street, and I lay there crying, shocked, still holding the veil in my hands. Slowly I got to my feet and watched as the procession continued out to Calvary. I could not follow. I could not move, for all my hopes had passed from me. I walked slowly to my house. There I realized that the veil in my hands felt different. It was no longer wool but some fine material. I looked at it, and it was silk!

"'Just then my father entered the house. He was yelling with joy. "See?" he said. "See what your Jesus is now? He is just a charlatan, a magician! You will now marry according to my wishes." He continued with his insults and finally demanded that I try on the bridal veil.

"'When I showed him the veil, he demanded to know where the one he had purchased was. I told him what had taken place. Then I showed him the veil. He did not believe me, and he beat me and threw me out of his house.'

"'Your father is a hard man. I don't understand his thinking,' stated Mary the wife of Cleophus. 'Surely he had seen that you were cured, and surely he knew that so great a thing would bring you to spiritual promises. Could he not see that the veil was no longer wool but silk? He had to believe all you said. I do not understand.'

"'He would not believe me.' The girl broke from Mary's embrace and walked away from the group. It appeared she was going to leave them. She stopped and with bowed head turned to the group of ladies.

"'I tell you the truth. My father believes I always lie. I did make a promise to my mother. I did wipe the face of Jesus, and as you can see the cloth did turn to silk. I speak the truth. Maybe it was too much for my father to understand, but you will understand. Jesus even wanted me to be able to prove my truthfulness. Look what He did.' She unfolded the veil before her, and there imprinted on it was a face.

"The women gasped in horror, for the face was distorted and ugly. It looked like the face of Longinus! But then they all grew calm. One by one they smiled, for they saw that it was the face of Jesus Christ. All the ugliness was gone, before them was beauty."

Nonna stopped again. She took a bite of the hot pepper, and I with no hesitation followed her. She got up from her chair, went slowly to the kitchen sink, drew water, slowly walked back to the table, and placed the glass before me. Just in time! For I had bitten into hell and all its punishing fires!

Calmly she began cleaning up. She gathered the crumbs from the table into her hand and walked out to the backyard to give them, as she always did, to the birds. She left me to my suffering. When she returned to the house, she looked at me, with tears in my eyes as a result of the hot pepper.

She calmly said, "Ugly is not on the face of a person. Ugliness is really in not knowing truth. When we know truth, we always know beauty."

She looked at me. "The pepper hot?"

I could not answer; my body was on fire. It would stay with me for days.

"Just now I was ugly with you by letting you eat that hot pepper. I was only thinking of punishing you. You see, even grown-ups can turn beauty and truth into ugly and lies."

She cleared her throat. She was unhappy that she had hurt me. She fidgeted with her apron. Looking at the tabletop she said, "You see, Vincenzo, truth when spoken always puts you in the presence of God."

She wiped her mouth with the end of her apron. "Ugly is not forever, for ugly can turn to beauty when you know the true person." She raised her eyes and looked directly at me.

"Lies keep you from achieving many things, for lies carry histories with them: your history. A person's history should be filled with truth and beauty. There is no room for ugly and lies. Do you understand this? No, of course not. Let me make it easier for you.

"Remember, even in the ugliest of times—the Crucifixion—there was beauty. He was God! He was beauty! He was truth!"

Thirteen

$\mathcal{L}$et's Make It Good

One day my grandmother and I went to the Italian grocery store on the corner of our street. This was one of my favorite places because the store had two huge porcelain basins of green and black olives preserved in hot pepper and olive oil. These two foods were my favorites, and on these visits I would sneak and have my fill of both these delicacies.

The owner of the store, whose name was Vincent but who for some unknown reason was called Jimmy, would often give me glares of disapproval yet never openly reproached me. So I just had my feasts.

On one particular day a tall, well-groomed man entered the store. All the other customers seemed to back away, and I knew something was happening that I was too young to understand. My grandmother immediately grabbed me, pulled me to her side, and placed her protective left hand around me.

The tall man walked about the store, surveying or pontificating, so it seemed. He walked with his coat draped over his shoulder, his wide-brimmed black hat cocked just slightly on his head, his shoes shined to a blinding sparkle. As he walked around the store he waved his hand back and forth, up and down, as if giving blessings to everything in the store. He spotted me and smiled widely.

"And who is this Irish-looking boy?" he asked in Italian.

My grandmother pulled me closer to her and, with the bravery of a peasant mother, said proudly, "He is my grandson, and he is all Italian."

"Ah! and one of the beautiful ones, it seems. Blond, light-skinned Italians with blue eyes are the most beautiful." He reached down and pinched my cheek. It really hurt.

"What is your name, grandson?"

"Vincenzo," Nonna said quickly, pulling me even more closely to her.

"Hmm, what a beautiful name!" He stood erect. "Am I right, Jimmy?"

"Si, Don Vincenzo," the grocer quickly replied.

"What would you like to have in this store?"

"Olives!" I yelled before my grandmother could speak for me or smother me with her grip.

"What kind?"

"Green and black," I replied with a wide grin.

"So it is. Jimmy, give this grandson a bag of each. Free."

"Si, Don Vincenzo."

"Of course!" the man replied, walking to the counter and slipping a piece of paper to Jimmy. "Here are the things we need. Have them delivered right away, and put them on my account."

"Si, Don Vincenzo, si."

"That's good." Looking at me one more time, he said, "And you, Irish boy, be good to your family and enjoy the olives, but be careful. Olives make Italians passionate for life and love."

My grandmother, in a tone slightly touched by displeasure, said to me, "Say thank you to the man, Vincenzo."

"Thank you, Mister," I said happily in Italian.

He extended his hand to me, but my grandmother immediately grabbed it away and kissed it. He then extended his hand to the others in the store, and they all kissed his hand. As he neared the door, he spun around with a great flair, gestured to all in the store, and was gone.

After his departure silence filled the store, but the place was alive with gestures: the shaking of heads, fists, and fingers, and glances that are known and understood by Italians only and that always say more than words.

Finally the silence was broken by unkind words: "trash," "leach," "parasite," and other more descriptive terms. But I didn't care—I had my olives!

On the way home I spoke excitedly about what had happened. I was happy, for I had two bags of olives. I somehow felt I was contributing to the family, for these goods would be shared by all.

My grandmother remained silent. Several times she showed signs of understanding and enjoying my excitement, but most of the time she remained silent. When we arrived home my excitement subsided, as I realized my grandmother's total lack of enthusiasm meant more than I could understand.

"What's wrong?" I asked her.

"Not everything is as it seems. You are happy over your olives, but poor Jimmy, the grocer, has lost money over the demands of that bully Don Vincenzo. You probably think this Don Vincenzo is a good man, but he is not. What you saw today was not goodness; what you saw today was fear, humiliation, and robbery."

My heart dropped. My excitement disappeared.

"Should I return these?" I asked, lifting the bags to her and hoping she would say it was not necessary.

"No, what happened today has nothing to do with you. You are a child and innocent. But remember, when you are dealing with God, or God is dealing with you, bad can produce good."

Nonna realized I was lost.

"Confused? Come let us have some olives, bread, and coffee."

Out came the cups, the milk, the brown sugar (it was still wartime), the dishes, and the olives. We sat.

"An old story, written by a great Italian writer, goes like this: Before Jesus was sentenced to die, Pilate was still a little confused and a little cowardly, so he had Jesus put in jail for a short time so he could think of what to do with Him. The cell Jesus was in was between the cell of Barabbas and the cell of the two thieves, Dismas and Gestas.

"While in his cell, Jesus prayed. They say an angel came and stayed with Him. It probably was Raphael, for he is 'the medicine of God.' Well, anyway, the cell that Jesus was in became filled with an unusually bright light, and that light shined through a small window in the wall of the two adjacent cells.

"Now, when Barabbas saw the light, he thought that it was a new day. He thought quickly to himself, *This is the day I shall die,* and with no fear in his heart he ignored the light.

"Gestas, the bad thief, thought it was a lantern. He quickly thought to himself, *I hope this jail burns to the ground,* and he also ignored the light.

"Dismas, the good thief, was not sure what it was, so he decided to look and see what was going on. So he climbed up the wall and looked into Jesus' cell. All he saw was a man huddled in the corner with his face buried in his hands. There was no lantern or torch or any light in the cell; the cell was in total darkness. The man in the corner was mumbling to himself.

"Dismas first thought, *He's a madman.* But because he had nothing else to do and because he could not understand where the light had come from, he decided to watch for a few more seconds.

"The prisoner raised His head, and His face was a pure, radiant, blinding light, which filled the room. Just as quickly the light was gone, and an ugly, badly beaten, bloody face was all that was left.

"Well, you know what happened. Barabbas was set free, and the two thieves were crucified with Jesus. When they were on the cross, Gestas began to curse Jesus because He was not helping him as He had helped others. To Gestas Jesus was a waste, a fake.

"Dismas, on the other hand, was silent. He was confused. All during the walk to the Mount, while the three of them were carrying their crosses, he had kept looking back at the face of Jesus. He had seen all of its broken features, all the spit, and the blood and the dirt that was on it. After Jesus was nailed to the cross and lifted up, Dismas looked again at His face.

"Where was the light? Had he imagined it the night before? Then Dismas heard Jesus ask His Father to forgive His killers. Suddenly Jesus' face glowed as it had in the cell. It was blinding, and all the blood and bruises and dirt and ugliness disappeared.

"Now Dismas understood that Jesus was innocent. So he yelled for Gestas to be silent, and he turned back to Jesus' blinding face and said, 'My Lord, remember me when You come into Your Kingdom.'

"Jesus turned His head to the Good Thief and said, 'Amen, Amen, I say to you, this day you will be with Me in Paradise.'

"Suddenly Jesus' face was no longer blinding, but all His handsome features returned. Dismas was in awe of the miracle he was witnessing. He gave thanks for being there. Dismas felt a deep happiness and calmness within himself and he felt a glow on his own face. He knew a miracle was taking place inside him.

"They say that Jesus died with a smile on His face because of Dismas' conversion. After all, isn't that why Jesus came into the world, to save souls? He must have truly been happy because He knew He had saved one soul. Can you imagine, Vincenzo, what a scene it was when Jesus returned home to His Father with a thief as His companion?"

I just sat in my kitchen chair. The question and the scene she had created were beyond any answer that I could give.

"Now, what does all this mean? When Dismas was caught by the Romans, that was bad for him. But if he had not been caught, he would not have been saved by Jesus, so it was good for him. If Dismas had not looked at Jesus and seen the bad things that had been done to Jesus' face, he would not have found joy in the light or in seeing Jesus' face miraculously glowing. Only from God does something bad become good.

"But also remember something: Even after Jesus promised Dismas heaven, Dismas had to suffer. They broke his legs, and he had to die by suffocation. But they say when they took Dismas' body from the cross, he also was smiling. Why? Because he was in Paradise and once again was seeing Jesus' face as a bright light."

She cleared her throat and took a sip of coffee to ease the dryness of her mouth.

"This man who gave you the olives was not a good thief. He stole from a good man and gave to you. He insulted Jimmy in front of all his customers, just as the bad thief did to Christ. Nothing good came from what happened today."

"But we have olives!"

"Yes, but we got them from something bad. We must make it good. So, Vinzee, a lesson: if ever you see a bad thing in this world, you must try to make it good, just as Dismas did. So tomorrow we will make something good of a bad thing."

The next day we went to the grocery store again. I was secretly hoping Don Vincenzo would be there, but he wasn't. Nonna ordered some canned goods, and Jimmy got them off the shelf. When it came time to pay, I saw my grandmother give Jimmy a five-dollar bill. Jimmy rang the register and gave Nonna her change.

"Jimmy," my Grandmother said loudly in Italian, "what are you doing? I gave you a dollar bill, and you gave me all this money back."

"No, Domenica," Jimmy protested, "you gave me a five."

"No. It was a one." She looked down at me.

I must have looked amazed. "Nonna, you gave ..."

She coughed and squeezed my shoulder.

"Jimmy, don't make me a bad thief." Again she looked down at me with a small grin and a twinkle in her eyes. "Vinzee, didn't I give him one dollar?"

I reached for her hand. Now I knew what she was doing. I knew it was something good, something right. I wanted to be a part of it. I remembered Nonna's story of Dismas, and I began to feel good all over. This is how Dismas felt!

"Yes, Nonna. You gave him one dollar."

She squeezed my hand to show her approval. "Here, Jimmy." She pushed the money back to the grocer. "Let's make it good."

Jimmy protested and argued, but the deed was done. We left the store with change for a one-dollar bill.

Years later, on the day my grandmother died, my family received several large bags of green and black olives from Jimmy the grocer. When he came to the viewing, he sought me out, kissed me, and said, "Your grandmother did something once that I shall never forget.

"You remember the thing about the olives and the five-dollar bill? She could never have given me a one-dollar bill, Vincenzo. I had no five- or ten-dollar bills in the cash register that morning until she came in and gave me the five-dollar bill. I gave her change for the five because that is what she gave me. Ah, but many days later I remembered the thing with Don Vincenzo and the olives. She was paying for his evil. I never was that close to so great a person as your grandmother."

He fought back the tears.

"You were her constant companion, and you loved her very much. You must always remember her and the things she did." He hugged and kissed me and whispered, "Vincenzo, I bet that five dollars bought her heaven."

Yeah, she was the Good Thief.

Fourteen

ℳy Work Is My Prayer

In the 1940s everywhere we went we saw more and more men and even some women in military uniforms. Some neighborhoods had been stripped of all their young men. We would pass houses that had a small rectangular flag hanging in the window. A wide red border surrounded a white square in the center, all edged with gold silky embroidery. On the white square was a blue star or stars that indicated a father, husband, or son in the Armed Services. It was common to see houses with more than one blue star. One family on my street had five blue stars.

Some unfortunate houses had a silver star on their flag, indicating their serviceman had been wounded, or a sadder gold star, which meant their serviceman had been killed in action. In my neighborhood there were four houses with gold stars and seven with silver.

Every morning the women—wives, mothers, sisters, aunts, girlfriends—would get up early, well before dawn, and prepare to go to work in factories that made things of war to destroy homes, kill or maim the enemy, but save our servicemen.

Every morning the daily Masses at our church were crowded with mothers, wives, sisters, daughters, and girlfriends praying for their servicemen. Churches had never been so crowded for daily Mass.

Every morning we children went to our schools, stood in the cold wind or warm sun, and watched the Stars and Stripes be raised to the top of a tall silver flagpole. We sang "The Star-Spangled Banner" or said the Pledge of Allegiance. America in the 1940s was saturated with patriotism.

Some neighborhoods collected money and purchased large banners that hung across the center of the street. The number of stars on these banners showed the total number of men and women from that city block who were serving in the Armed Services. My street had such a banner. I cannot remember the total number of stars, although I am sure it was over forty.

From time to time the Civilian Defense Corps, composed mostly of women, the elderly, and ineligible draftees, would have neighborhood drives. We were asked to collect and contribute paper, rubber goods, and metal items. We heaped them in a big pile at the end of our city block, and these things would be picked up by the Corps' trucks, to be recycled for the war effort.

The paper donations were never a problem, because we would save all our newspapers, brown paper bags, old advertisements, and any other paper product and heap them on the pile. The rubber drives were more of a challenge, because most of us didn't have that many rubber products. But somehow we found old car tires, new and old bike tires, rubber garden hoses, and other good and new things to throw on the pile.

The biggest hardship was the metal drive. A lot of valuable things were given away that had both material and sentimental value. Old bikes from someone's bygone youth, old wagons from bygone fun, old tire rims from bygone travels, and old pots and pans of bygone family meals were a few of the things that were heaped in the pile at the end of our street.

Just before one of these "junk drives" a few of our neighbors had received some bad news. A young son of one of our neighbors, who was exceptionally well-liked, was killed in action, and two other families received word that their sons had been wounded in combat. The entire neighborhood went into mourning, very saddened by what had taken place. Even we kids, out of respect, stopped playing in the street and tried to be as quiet as possible.

Now, Nonna had few favorite things in her life. Among these few favorites were two iron skillets in which she cooked our family meals. One was a very large skillet, so large that she could fry eight eggs or twelve to fifteen large meatballs in it at one time. The other skillet was smaller and would do only half that amount of food at a time.

On the day of the "junk drive" I walked into the kitchen and saw Nonna carefully remove the large skillet from the gas range and wipe it down slowly, with great reverence and love. She held it in her hands for the longest time, looking at it with a serious face. Finally she smiled widely and put the skillet on the gas range.

"How is the metal drive going?" she asked.

"It seems people are giving away a lot more stuff than ever before," I answered.

"That's good," she said.

That night, I walked into the kitchen and saw Nonna cooking supper for us on the small skillet. I watched for the longest time as she finished frying some potatoes and then had to fry some more. I was confused as to why she didn't use the large skillet and get the potatoes fried more quickly.

"Nonna, why don't you use the large pan? You'll get done faster," I said.

"I don't have the large skillet anymore. I gave it to the metal drive this afternoon."

"But, Nonna, that was one of your favorite things."

"So who needs favorite things? Besides, we used that pan only once in a while. Maybe now someone will be able to use it more often, or maybe it will save the life of some poor soldier or sailor. I still can do the same things with the smaller pan."

"But now you will have to work twice as hard," I said somewhat selfishly, for that meant she would be in the kitchen longer and not able to talk to me so often.

She turned from the gas range and looked at me.

"I want you to sit over there and listen to me.

"One day the mother-in-law of St. Peter was washing her family clothes at the nearby stream. Jesus came along. Seeing that she was scrubbing the clothes on a small stone, He became a little confused. This was doing things the hard way. The poor old woman was working much harder than she should.

"He said to her, 'Mother, why are you washing your clothes and beating them on a small stone and not on a larger stone?'

"The woman looked up. Smiling she replied, 'The smaller stone makes my task longer, and therefore my work, which is my prayer, takes longer. Using the smaller stone makes my conversation and visit with God a bit longer. I don't need less time with God, so I use the smaller rock.'

"Jesus just smiled and walked away.

"So," Nonna said, "as my work is my prayer, now I'll spend more time talking to God."

I smiled and walked away.

Fifteen

$\mathcal{B}$ ad Things Always Follow You Around

"One day the King of the Beasts, the mightiest of all the Lions, called all the animals in the world to an important assembly. He, the King of the Beasts, had decided it was time to rearrange the Ruling Council of Animals. He had decided to make it more universal and therefore to permit other animals on the Council instead of just the members of the Cat Family. This decision made the outgoing members of the Council (the tigers, leopards, cheetahs, and panthers) very angry, but none of them would dare to speak up for fear of the King of the Beasts.

"The King of the Beasts opened the assembly to nominations. The Whale was first chosen because his jumping in and out of the water made waves in the ocean, and the King of the Beasts thought that was a good thing. The Eagle was then chosen because he was able to fly high and keep an eye on the things that were happening in the world. Next chosen was the Dog because he was the best friend anyone could have, and then the Lamb because Jesus was called that by John the Baptist. The Elephant came next because he was so big and strong. And, next to last, the Hyena was chosen to keep all members of the Council laughing.

"The members of the Cat Family were totally disappointed

because none of them had been chosen. So they decided to stop all nominations for the last position on the Council unless it was a member of the Cat Family. Every animal that was nominated from that moment on was loudly condemned. The cats denounced all the nominees by making up lies and concocting stories. Each time this happened the King of the Beasts would veto the nomination.

"Finally the King of the Beasts said, 'I would like to see a member of the Horse Family on my Council. They have been helpful to all for many years. I think they should be rewarded for this.'

"The Rhinoceros spoke up and with much gusto nominated the Zebra.

"Immediately the Cat Family began to find things wrong with the Zebra. 'They are not fast enough,' they said, 'and they don't do anything. They just eat grass and run, and they don't speak the same as the other horses.'

"The King of Beasts scratched the dirt and tossed up a flair of dust, and everyone knew the nomination was dead.

"Then the wise old Owl nominated the Mule. The Cat Family was stunned. They huddled together with hopes of destroying the nomination, but they could not find anything wrong with the Mule.

"The wise old Owl began to give his reasons. 'The Mule,' he said, 'carried Mary and the Christ Child to Bethlehem.'

"This quickly got the King's interest.

"Then the wise old Owl added, 'When Jesus was in trouble, the Mule carried Him to safety into Egypt.'

"The King purred with delight.

"Finally the wise old Owl said, 'And when Jesus was at His

highest moment, it was the Mule who carried Jesus into Jerusalem in triumph.'

"The King raised his head majestically and with great pride acknowledged the good deeds of this animal of his Kingdom.

"Now the Cat Family knew they had lost. They could not possibly say anything against the Mule, not with all those great achievements and credentials.

"The King waited a few moments and then with a mighty voice finally spoke.

"'With these credentials the Mule must be appointed to the Council.'"

"And with an even mightier commanding voice he declared, 'Let the Mule come forward.'

"The Mule came slowly to the throne. His head, normally bowed, was lifted high with pride.

"'You and the members of your family have done well. I approve of your appointment to the final seat on the Council.'"

"With a roar from his mighty mouth the appointment was confirmed, and all the animals cheered their approval.

"Then the Giraffe, who had just arrived at the Assembly, asked to say something from his many lofty thoughts.

"'I am not as swift as the Horse, Your Majesty, nor am I as smart as the Owl, nor am I as hateful as the members of the Cat Family, but I think you should reconsider this last appointment.'

"The King of the Beasts was annoyed. He could not take the appointment back; it was not permitted. He swiftly turned his head to the Giraffe, whom he had rewarded many years before with the gifts of sophistication and solemnity because of his ability to see great distances and foretell things to come—and because of his aloofness.

"'Why should I reconsider?' the King demanded angrily.

"'Well, you see, Your Majesty,' replied the Giraffe very slowly, 'it was the Mule who, after the tree was cut down, carried that tree into Jerusalem.'

"'So, ... so,' prodded the King with some annoyance and impatience, for it was time for his afternoon nap and this Assembly was taking too long, and his patience was worn thin.

"'The tree was used to make the cross that was carried by Jesus and on which He was crucified.' The Giraffe cleared his long throat and raised his head high above all the Assembly and said with great elegance, 'I saw this all with my own eyes.'

"The entire Assembly gasped.

"The Cats purred and clawed the dirt.

"The King slumped back on his throne.

"'But, Your Majesty,' said the Mule in quick defense, 'that was only one of our kind. This mule you speak of is unknown to the rest of us. We don't even know his name. The rest of us have been the beast of burden to Mankind for centuries.'

"The Assembly began to murmur that they wanted a recall of the appointment.

"'You cannot take back an appointment,' said the wise old Owl. 'It is not proper. It is against all our laws.'

"'A recall is unheard of, Your Majesty, and it would cause great problems and uncertainty in the Kingdom and in your reign,' added the well-educated Bookworm, who had been the King's chief adviser for many years.

"'But look what the Mule has done,' roared the Cats. 'Recall the appointment! Give it to one of us!'

"'No!' thundered the King. 'What has been done cannot be undone.'

"He closed his eyes and thought for a moment. With his sharp claws he slowly combed his mighty mane. Everyone fell silent, for they knew that this was a bad sign.

"Finally he opened his eyes and, with a voice filled with strength and great authority, roared, 'The appointment will stand!'

"He raised his head higher and looked at the Mule with fury in his eyes. The Mule cowered in his place. All in the Assembly moved back a step in fear.

"'But, Brother Mule,' he stated, 'henceforth all the members of your family will not be so willing to help mankind. You shall become obstinate and difficult, and you shall be disliked for this stubbornness, and you will be regarded as stupid.'

"He paused to control his temper and to add drama to his next decree.

"'Furthermore, I decree that he who carried this tree shall be known to all as "He Hauled," and you and your like shall forevermore call out to all in my Kingdom and to all humans his disgrace—this name.'

"That is why, still today, a mule bays, 'Hee-haw.'"

Sixteen

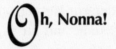h, Nonna!

During the War, when factories were booming and in high production, employees of these factories were being pushed to the limits. No one complained because it was all for the war effort. Nonna helped by babysitting her six grandchildren while her daughters and daughter-in-law were working in various factories. But this wasn't enough for Nonna. She began "doing coats" at home.

The clothing factories were swamped with government contracts for clothing for our servicemen and servicewomen. To help keep up with these demands the management of the factories sought out people who were tailors who could work from their houses, sewing and basting uniforms or civilian coats and jackets. Those who did this kind of "piece work" were paid by the coat or uniform completed. It wasn't big money, but what was important for Nonna and others was that they felt they were contributing.

So once a week a man named Bruno from the nearby clothing factory would deliver seventy-five to eighty coats or uniforms to our house. A week later he would come back to pick up the completed coats. When these deliveries were made, we grandchildren would begin to grumble because we were expected to help with the sewing.

Some of us had to thread the sewing needles so as to save Nonna's time, and others were taught how to sew. The latter each had a part to do: the back, collar, sleeve, or underarm. Others had to clean the coats of any threads or debris.

My job was the underarm basting, and Nonna taught me well. I was a speed demon and an expert at it. One time Nonna decided I should broaden my horizons and do the collar. That was a disaster, so I became the permanent underarm baster in our small group of tailors.

Tailoring was an art that Nonna made us proud to share with her. "Look at your mothers and aunts and some of your uncles. They know how to sew. It is something you should know how to do so you can repair your own clothes and the clothes of your families if ever you have to do such a thing," she would say. We obeyed, and we never regretted learning how to sew.

During the day when we grandchildren were in school, Nonna would get all her housework done. She would do her cleaning, washing, ironing, and some cooking, and wait for us to come home from school. When time neared for us to arrive, Nonna would sit and begin sewing some coats. We would arrive home and do what was expected of us. We contributed without resistance, though we hated the idea and regretted the time we had to spend sewing rather than playing.

We would gather in a circle, with the coats piled high in the center of us and we would pick up a partially finished coat and do our part of the job. To make the time pass and to make things a little more pleasant, Nonna would teach us Italian songs, and we would have a sing-a-long. She would also talk to us about our family tree and explain how this or that person was related to us. With our extended family as big as it was, it was good to know where everyone fit in the puzzle. She would tell us Italian folk tales, and more often she would tell us about her hometown in Italy. She told us the following story so often that we knew every part of it by memory, and we could envision the town very easily.

Nonna was from a small village in Italy. The town when she lived in it had about two thousand people. It had one big church called "Our Lady of the Countryside" and two small *cappelles* (chapels) churches. Our Lady of the Countryside was the patroness of the town. Every town in Italy, no matter its size, has a patron saint.

Her hometown was built on a small hill. Four large roads came from the four directions of the compass and went up the hill to the Piazza de Madonna in the center of town. Apparently most people entered her town from the east. Her father and his family were shepherds who grazed their sheep just east of town. A number of the buildings in the town were stores, but there were many family dwellings also. A majority of the people lived on the outskirts of the town on farms.

"If you come in from the east side of my town, the first building you saw was the fish store. This store was owned by one of my mother's distant cousins. Across the road from the fish store was the butcher who, I am told, once wanted to marry one of my aunts. But my grandparents, your great-great grandparents, didn't like his family, so they matched my aunt up with another man.

"Next door to the butcher was a candlestick-maker who also sold kerosene lamps and kerosene, and next door to the candle shop was the bakery. My girlfriend lived next door to the bakery, and her house was always warm because of the baker's oven. She also has come to America. After that came the houses of the people who lived in my town. On the other sides of the town were the other stores.

"Everyone in town used to know each other. I knew all of your grandfather's sisters and brothers. It was such a nice feeling to know everyone in town. It made us all one family, and when one person was in trouble or sick or dying, the whole town would get together and help out.

"In the center of the town, in the Piazza de Madonna, is the beautiful statue of my town's patroness, Our Lady of the Countryside. Her face is so real-looking, and she is so beautiful. On her feast day the townspeople dress the statue up with real clothing. The best silk and velvet are used, and sometimes pearls and other gems are sewn on her clothing. She is crowned with an expensive crown, and we townspeople sing and pray for her intercession.

"The statue is high on a pedestal that is part of a water fountain, and this fountain produces sapphire blue water; it is the most beautiful water you ever would see. People from the nearby villages would come to my hometown and look at this water in amazement. No one had ever seen sapphire blue water, and many believed it was a miracle."

When she would finish telling us this story, she would seem so proud, yet there was some sadness in her eyes. For after she came to America, she never saw her parents again. We knew that bothered her.

On the other hand, we would sigh with relief when the story was over—told again, in fact, every time we sat down to "do coats." This story of the water fountain was imbedded in our memories.

Many years later, long after Nonna died, one of my aunts was going to Italy. She told me she and her husband were going to drive through Nonna's district and province and possibly visit the town. I told her if she entered the east side of town she would see the fish store, the bakery, the butcher store, and the candle store. She listened to me politely but didn't, I was sure, have much confidence in my story. I also told her of the statue in the middle of the town and of the miraculous blue water.

Many months after my aunt's return I was able to see her and talk about her trip. I finally asked her about Nonna's hometown.

"My God, Vince, what an eerie feeling I got when I entered the town and found the stores exactly as you had said they were. How did you know that?"

"Nonna told us all about them when we were 'doing coats.' It was her way of keeping us calm and working. How about the statue of the Virgin? Was that as I said?"

"Oh, goodness, yes. She looks so real, and she is so very beautiful."

"And the water? Was it as sapphire blue as I said it would be?"

"Of course," my aunt said with a wide smile. I almost sighed with contentment and happiness, for the image I had of the town was validated.

"It had to be," my aunt continued. "They paint the bottom of the fountain sapphire blue."

Oh, Nonna!

Seventeen

$\mathcal{F}$inding New Things in Each Other

There was a boy in my classes at King of Peace school who was very quiet and shy and kept to himself all the time. He and I became friendly, mostly because I felt sorry for him but also because I felt very comfortable with him. He was a good listener, and we shared a lot of things in common.

One day I asked him if he wanted to come to my neighborhood and meet my other friends. I was hoping he would make more friends and maybe become a part of my neighborhood group. He responded with great excitement, so the next day he came to my neighborhood. But soon I realized his visit was a mistake; he remained very quiet, and when asked something he would give quick, one-word answers.

The next day in school he confirmed what I had suspected. He told me that my friends didn't seem to like him and made him feel unwelcome. Than he asked me to come to his neighborhood and join in play with his friends.

I felt a little uncomfortable with his suggestion because he lived many city blocks away from my house, but I agreed. When I arrived in his neighborhood, I discovered that all his friends were much older than I was. They were not so nice to younger kids, so I withdrew from the games and just watched. The next day he said he knew I didn't have a good time, and he apologized for his friends.

For days after our exchanged visits I was confused. I could not understand why we didn't fit in with each other's friends. I could not figure out how two friends could not have mutual friends and then be complete friends in everything. I needed some answers and some understanding, so I went to Nonna for some help.

I found her in the kitchen making a birthday cake for her daughter, my aunt. She was deeply engrossed in the cake when I arrived. I leaned over the table and watched her pour the homemade cake batter into the baking pan.

"So what's wrong?" she asked. I was always surprised whenever she asked this question, because she seemed to know when I was troubled. I was certain she could read minds or had some magical powers or was blessed by God with greater insight than the rest of us.

"Oh, nothing," I replied, not wanting to appear too anxious to seek her wisdom.

"Hmm, so Adam and Eve said when God asked what they wanted."

She placed the baking pan in the oven and whispered to me, "Be quiet." Every time she would bake a cake or make bread, we were all told to be quiet because the cake might "fall" or the bread would not rise.

"If you promise to be still and quiet, we will have a small cup of coffee and talk about what is troubling you. Agree? Good. You stay where you are, and I will get things ready for a cup of coffee."

After she had quietly gotten all the things together, I told her the problem I was having. She looked at me with sadness in her eyes.

"Sometimes people are not meant to be together. I remember reading a story by St. Francis that showed why this is so. Would you like to hear it?"

"Sure, Nonna," I said happily and with some relief, for now I would understand why things got all messed up.

"One day the Polar Bear decided to visit his old friend the Grizzly Bear. He arrived in the forest, and within minutes the hunters began shooting at him because his white fur could be seen for miles around. They chased him and chased him, until finally he ran to his friend's cave, packed his belongings, and went home to the North Pole.

"Sometime later the Grizzly decided that if it was unsafe for his friend to come and stay in the forest, maybe it would be better if he visited his friend at the North Pole. So he packed his bags and left for the North Pole. Within minutes of his arrival he began to be chased by the other polar bears, who thought he was a strange or sick bear that should not be with them. They made fun of him and chased him. So he packed all his belongings and returned to the forest.

"The next day the Grizzly Bear wrote his friend and said, 'Write me when you can, but I'll stay here where I know everything, and you stay there where you know everything. Someday soon we will meet at a place where neither of us knows anything. We will learn new things and together grow closer. Then we can be better friends.'"

She smiled and pushed a few homemade Italian biscuits across the table to me.

"So, you see, sometimes no matter what we do, things don't fit together. It takes a lot of understanding to make different things work. Friendship is founded on what people have in common with each other, not what they want others to find. Stay friendly with your schoolmate, but don't try to find common ground with old things in your lives. Instead try to find new things in each other."

Eighteen

Small People Do Big Things for Love

Christmas is time for "La Famiglia" (The Family). It is a time of children, of birth, and of innocence. It is a time for family gatherings, with the idea of making something different happen, in celebration of a time when a different thing did happen: the birth of the Son of God.

My grandmother was good at making Christmas different. For days before Christmas she would be in the kitchen baking Italian pizzelles, biscotto, and cookies. The oven's heat warmed the entire house, and the good smells filled it. Our taste buds would perk up, but tasting these special treats was forbidden until Christmas Eve. The entire family waited with anticipation for the feast that was to come.

My grandmother had created a title for Mary that I believe no other person had ever given her. Whenever Nonna was in the middle of cooking anything for her family, she always spoke of Mary and invoked the title "Santa Maria di Nazaret"— St. Mary of Nazareth. One time out of curiosity I asked my grandmother about this title, and she replied, "Mary is the Protectress of the Kitchens. She cooked for the Son of God in her humble kitchen with poor pots and pans—nothing fancy."

I remember often sitting in the kitchen watching and smelling the batter being turned, stirred, folded, and kneaded. Nonna would make small hissing sounds as she worked her batter. I was sure this was a requirement for being a good baker. Years later I asked her why she made this hissing sound, and she told me she was praying and asking Mary for her help.

"The Blessed Mother was a very good cook," she said. "It was her cooking that made Jesus grow into a strong man, and you never hear of Joseph or Jesus not liking what she cooked. No great writer has ever said that anyone in the Holy Family starved or got sick from bad cooking. All young brides and mothers and old grandmothers should ask Mary for help when they are cooking."

How right she always was!

The other part of Christmas was also a very special one: the Italian tradition of "La Vigilia." "La Vigilia" is the Vigil of Christmas or the Christmas Eve celebration. This is the final day of preparation for Christmas. It was a meatless day. No one was permitted to even think of meat.

Early Christmas Eve morning, Nonna would wake very early, go to Mass, and then begin her day by baking fresh bread. I cannot explain the salivating effects this had on a boy my age. The rest of the day was spent frying fish and preparing for the big feast that evening.

The Vigil dinner consisted of cheese, fish, and macaroni. The cheese was served first to symbolize the milk of Mary, which nurtured the Christ Child. Then there were various types of fish. The number of fish eaten had to be one, three, seven, or nine, because these numbers had symbolic meanings in the Christmas story.

According to Nonna, one fish symbolized the Christ Child, and three symbolized the Holy Family—Jesus, Mary, and Joseph. Seven was symbolic of the Holy Family, the three shepherds, and all the choir of angels. And finally nine was the Holy Family, the three shepherds, and the Three Magi.

To make the Christmas Eve meal even more different, spaghetti was served without red gravy or sauce. It was boiled, and garlic fried in olive oil was poured over it. This was called Agli'olie, and it was a symbol of the pure white hair of the choir of angels.

One Christmas Eve day I was feeling very left out. I felt sorry for myself because I could not find anything to do to help out for "La Vigilia." I asked Nonna if I could help, and she told me to sit and watch. But this did not help me, because sitting and watching her made me feel even more useless.

She noticed and asked me what was wrong.

"I can't seem to do anything for La Vigilia," I answered.

"I'll tell you what," she said. "You pray while I cook."

"But that's not a big thing," I said, more frustrated than before.

"Ahh! So you only want to do big things," she said as she continued to flour one of the fish. "And who is supposed to do the little things?"

With that question she walked to the kitchen sink and washed the white flour off her hands.

She turned and said, "Sometimes the small things we do are bigger than all the big things. Do you understand that?"

Of course not! That's stupid! I thought.

"Let me tell you something," she said, walking to a kitchen chair. "Come here, and sit beside me."

And the story goes:

"Early one day, all the angels in the holy realm learned that heaven and earth were to be one because the Son of God was to be born as a Child, given to earth for a little while. The different choirs of angels began rehearsing their great songs of praise and glory. The messenger angels began to practice their proper speeches. Some of the archangels polished their armor, others fluffed their wings, still others combed their hair, and others shined their haloes.

"There remained a few small cherubim who found that they had nothing to do. They began going around asking for something to do, but all they did was bump into the other angels and get in everyone's way.

"Gabriel, seeing what was happening and needing to make things move along smoothly and quietly, called the smaller angels into his office and informed them that they had to find something to do this night to make it different from all other nights. He told them to sit in the corner and think of what they could do.

"So the small cherubs sat together and began to think. They thought for a long, long time. They had to find something to do. This was too important a night not to contribute something to it.

"Finally they thought, *If the others will be singing the good news to man of God's Son's birth, then we should tell the rest of creation of the good news.*

"One angel named Natural said, 'I will go and tell the hills, the mountains, and the seas.'

"*Good,* they all thought, *then the oldest things in the world would know also.*

"Another little angel named Friendly said, 'I will go and tell all the beasts and the animals of the world.'

"*Good,* they agreed, *then the companions of men will know.*

"And another angel named Clear said, 'I will go and tell the clouds to stay away.'

"They agreed that also was a great idea. Then the sky would be clear and open.

"And still another angel named Breeze said, 'I'll tell the wind to be still.'

"*Great,* they all agreed, *then the night will be silent.*

"Still another small angel named Shine said, 'I'll tell the moon to shine more brightly.'

"They all smiled for that also was a good idea; now the night would be bright.

"And finally the smallest of the angels, named Sparkle, said, 'I will tell the stars to twinkle.'

"*Ahh,* they agreed, *that would be the final touch.* Twinkling stars would speak to all the world.

"Suddenly they all felt a strong wind pass, and they all bowed down low. They knew He was with them.

"They then heard the words, 'You have pleased Me, little cherubs, for this night will be a holy time, and I will fill it with promises to all.'"

Nonna sat back in satisfaction and smiling said, "You see what little things can do?" She got up from her chair and walked to the gas range and began checking each of the frying fish. She looked at me over her shoulder with a wider smile on her face. She knew she had me.

"What else, Nonna?"

"What else? Don't you see? The little angels found those little things to do for the love of the Baby Jesus, and it is because of them that tonight we celebrate a silent night, a holy night, a night that is all calm and that is all bright."

So I just sat in the corner the rest of the day and prayed, and for some reason that Christmas everything on the dinner table tasted better than ever before.

$\mathcal{W}$e Will Make Jesus Smile

We were raised with a strong sense of respect for our elders, for authority, and for the property of others. If ever we failed to show respect toward any of these things, we were reprimanded strongly.

Up the street from my house was the home of a woman named Emma. It was common knowledge to everyone in the neighborhood that Emma, though she appeared old, was young. She had a bad heart. So everyone in the neighborhood would check in on her throughout the day. It was very common for neighbors, young and old alike, to walk by her house and, seeing her seated by the window in her big upright chair, stop and talk to her. We weren't even tempted to be unkind or disrespectful to her, because she was a very kind and happy lady even in her illness. I was one of her favorite people, and often she would invite me into her house so that we could talk.

Many hours of my playtime were spent talking and even doing homework in Emma's house. Her husband, Joe, worked all day, and I sometimes would wait for him to arrive home before leaving Emma. I noticed that when he came home from work he tended to his wife's needs. He would cook, clean, and wash clothes. This was long before men were expected to do these things, and he did it willingly and with great love.

During one particular Lent, the Franciscan Sisters in our school asked us to do extra special things for our neighbors, especially those whose husbands and sons were away at war. They suggested running errands, taking out the trash, sweeping their steps, and even cleaning their houses.

I procrastinated on this project for reasons I now cannot remember, and when I finally got around to offering to do something for my neighbors, I found that the other children in the neighborhood had already volunteered their help. I was angry with myself for waiting so long. Lent would start the next day. I walked down my street dejectedly.

Suddenly, as I passed by Emma's house, I suspected that no one had asked to help her and Joe because they had no children in the War. So I made a quick charge to their house before someone else had the same thought as I had.

Emma invited me in, and I instantly offered her my services.

"Oh, no, Vincent, Joe and I are doing just fine. We don't need any help," she said quickly.

I was at a loss. I knew they could use my help, for I had seen Joe come home from work tired and do all the chores in the house. I decided to return that night and talk to Joe. But first I had to talk to Nonna, for I was sure she would give me some ammunition to persuade him. And she did.

"Well, it is important for you to understand that that nice lady Emma is a very proud woman, and I am sure her husband is just as proud. He is doing all those things out of love for his wife, and if he gives you some of those things to do, it will be cutting in on his love for her. I don't know if you will get him to agree to your helping him." Nonna nodded her head in agreement with her analysis of the situation.

She looked at me and smiled. "But, Vincenzo, I am proud of you. It was very good of you to think of Emma and Joe, and in the long run I am sure they will never forget you for the kindness you have shown them." She looked at me for a long time, and I was sure she saw my disappointment.

"You know, I am sure if you give me time, I will be able to give you something that will help you change their minds. Give me a few minutes and come back." She bent down as I pecked her on the cheek.

"I'll give you ten minutes," I yelled as I scampered away.

I heard her laugh aloud at my generous offer.

Three minutes later I was back.

"Ten minutes already?" she said with a smile on her face. "Well, in my quick ten minutes," she continued, "I remembered a story about Jesus and His grandparents that might help you. Come, let's go in the kitchen, have coffee, and talk."

She led the way, and I eagerly followed her. We sat down, and she told me the story. I decided it would be perfect to use on Joe and Emma before we had our family supper. So just before suppertime I told my mother I had something to do that was very important, and I promised that I would be back in time for family supper. I left the house and ran down to Emma and Joe's house.

Joe answered the door and happily invited me into the house. He asked me to sit in one of the chairs near Emma.

"Emma was telling me about your offer to help, Vincent, and I really think it was very nice of you to remember us. But I have to agree with Emma and say 'Thank you but no.'"

"Joe, did Emma mention that this was a Lenten school project that the nuns thought would help all our neighbors, especially those families who have husbands or sons in the service?"

"Yes, she did, and we think it is a great idea. But I'm not in the service, and we have no children in the service. How about the many neighbors on the street who fit this bill? Have you asked them?"

"Yeah, and they are all taken," I said with great disappointment.

"Well, we are doing fine, and we really don't need any help," Joe said as he wiped his hands on the dishtowel he was holding.

"You know, you and Emma sound just like Ann and Joachim."

"Who?" Emma asked.

"Ann and Joachim. They were Jesus' grandparents."

They both looked at me as if I were insane, and I figured I had messed up even before I told them Nonna's story. Swallowing hard, I began.

"One day Jesus came across His grandparents walking up a steep dirt road just outside of Nazareth. St. Joachim and St. Ann, who were elderly, were holding each other's hands very tightly, as if they were supporting each other.

"Jesus immediately walked over to them and, extending His muscular arm, said, 'Here, Nanno and Nonna, let Me help you. This road is steep, and you seem to need My help.'

"St. Joachim looked at his grandson and smiling said, 'My dear grandson, I am not that old that I cannot hold up my wife, and she isn't that old that she cannot hold me. We are holding hands not to hold each other up but to conquer this steep road together. This road is another thing that is a part of life and living, and we, like all married people, will conquer this steep road as we have conquered other things in life. And as always with God's help we will succeed.'

"'Yes, I know,' Jesus said laughing, 'so accept My help.' And He helped them just a little.

"As they were walking up the steep road, St. Ann, who was breathing heavily, looked at her grandson and said, 'You made it so much easier. It was less wear and tear on our old tired bones. We couldn't have done it without Your help. Whatever energies You have helped us save, we will use for other things. Thank you.'

"Jesus smiled, as God always does when He is appreciated."

I looked at Emma and Joe, and they looked amazed. I knew I had them.

"So with God's help, let me help you, and we'll make Jesus smile," I added from my own thoughts.

"That's a beautiful story, Vincent. I suppose one of your nuns told it to you," Emma said with a small grin on her lips.

Nonna had told me not to tell them she told me the story, and I didn't want to lie because I respected them both. So I thought for a moment and saw my way out.

"Yes, one of my teachers told me the story," I said, happy that I did not lie.

"Joe?" Emma said, looking at her husband for direction.

Joe looked at me, and I held my breath. I remembered what Nonna had said, that by doing what I was doing I would be taking some of his love for Emma away from him. I uttered a quick prayer to Jesus, asking Him to make Joe realize that I would be adding to his love for Emma instead.

Joe lowered his head (I believed he was smiling), and I

heard him say, "What do you want to do first for your Ann and Joachim?"

I wanted to jump with joy but instead remained calm and said, "Tonight's trash night. I'll come back after supper and take your trash out for you."

"Good start," Joe said, looking up and extending his hand for me to shake it.

I shook his hand and then walked to Emma, whose face was beaming with glee. I leaned over, kissed her, and left for home, walking about five feet off the ground. When I walked into the house, my family was just getting ready to sit down to supper.

Nonna took one look at me and read the glee on my face. She smiled. Later, when she was washing the supper dishes, I walked into the kitchen.

"So you succeeded. Good!"

I told her every detail of what had happened. When I told her what I had added from my own thoughts, she looked at me with great happiness.

"Someday you will be a good storyteller," she said. She reached for a dishtowel and got one for me. Together we began drying the dishes.

"I've been thinking, Vinzee, some days I will help you. I can bake a cake for Emma and Joe and maybe make a good Italian meal for them. Then you and I will be doing good for Lent, and together we will make Jesus smile."

Twenty

*A*ngels Need Feathers to Fly

My grandmother had a great love of angels. I am certain it was because she was born on October 2, the feast day of the Guardian Angels. When I was very young, she would often talk to me about these mysterious beings who moved in and out of our lives. I had many questions about them.

"Nonna, is it true that angels talk to babies?" I had heard my married cousin make this statement several days before.

"Oh, yes! They talk to babies while the babies are sleeping. You can tell when an angel is talking to a baby because the baby will be smiling. Remember, the souls of babies are just moments away from God, and they are still blessed with the memory of being with Him.

"Angels talk to the babies and tell them about all the good things God created in life. They also tell them of the good things they can do to help others that will make God happy. They tell them how they can help spread God's Holy Word. And they always remind them of the promises of the good and holy things of heaven.

"Now, when babies cry in their sleep, it means that the angels are telling them they will soon forget having been with God, and soon angels will stop coming and speaking in their dreams. The angels do promise that they will always be with them and will watch over them at all times. They also tell babies of the bad and sad things in life that they must grow up with but stay away from.

"When a baby is not crying or not smiling and is just sleeping, his guardian angel is singing a lullaby to him. During these times the baby is calm and at peace, and the baby sleeps and grows strong. Angels are often talking to babies in their sleep, because things are new and still uncomplicated. As we grow, angels still visit us in dreams, but their visits are disguised and confusing, and we may not understand what they are saying. That is because the older we get the more complicated we get and the more confusing we make things."

"Do angels have names?"

"Of course they do. God gives them names that match what they do for Him in heaven."

"How can I get to know my angel's name?"

"You have to give your angel a name, a special name that means something to only you. But if you want to know the name God gave your angel, you should go to Church and listen. Give God a chance to speak to you. I bet you will hear a name. But don't be too surprised if the name God has for your angel is the same as your name."

One day later, after a busy day at school, I asked, "Nonna, today Sr. Mary Clara told my class that every time a church bell rings, all the angels in heaven come down to earth. Is that really true?"

"I believe that it is true. A wise man of God many years ago said that church bells have the same meaning to both people and angels. Bells are calls to remind us to praise God, and they are also alarms that tell us something is wrong. To me, I think these two things mean the same.

"In my hometown in Italy the church bells would ring to call the people together for an important piece of news. Many times the news was bad, so whenever I hear a church bell ringing, I know I should pray to God—either to praise and thank Him or to ask His protection from any bad news.

"You know, I think our church bells rang a lot of times. I remember they rang for baptisms, reminding the angels and us that another soul was claimed by God. When the bells rang for weddings, it told angels and us that love was found between two of God's servants.

"Church bells are rung at funerals to alert St. Peter that another soul is coming and to inform all the other angels that a guardian angel is coming home and taking another soul back to God. Then all the angels, saints, and loved ones of the person who died gather at the gates and wait for the pilgrim's return."

One day, after many confusing thoughts about God and angels, I asked her, "Nonna, if God is everywhere, why do we need angels?"

"Another wise-guy question? We need angels *because* God is everywhere. He is a busy Person. He moves the sun and moon in and out. He changes summer to autumn and autumn to winter. He talks to plants, trees, barley, wheat, and oats and tells them to grow. He moves icebergs away from ships and calms the sea so we can travel across it. He listens all day long to our prayers and questions and needs, and He answers every one of them.

"He does millions of things all day long—day in and day out. So having a little angel helping Him here and there gets things done faster. Angels answer to Him, and they are very obedient and don't ask Him questions. They just do.

"Let me surprise you. Human beings can also be angels. We are here to help one another. Human beings just do things, and they believe and they love and are loved back. Who knows, I might be one of your guardian angels!"

I looked at her in complete shock but quickly warmed to the idea. Nonna would be a great guardian angel. I liked to think about it.

"It's not so hard to believe, Vincenzo. I'm always answering your wise-guy questions, and that is giving God time to do other things. So maybe I should let you bother me more often, then God could get some things done and maybe rest more than one day."

On one of my frustrated days when I asked my guardian angel to help me pass a math test, I said to Nonna in disappointment, "I'm always talking to my angel, and he never says anything to me. I don't think he is always with me."

"Of course he is. God has given you an angel who will stay with you until you are called to be judged before Him. He never leaves your side, even when you don't want him there. I can see you don't believe me. Well, if you are still not sure you have a guardian angel, then just take a walk in the sunlight or in the moonlight. As you walk, you will see your angel on the ground before you or following you. So never think you are without an angel. Your guardian angel is always with you in the dark and in the light, in good places and in bad places."

Every picture I saw showed angels with big strong wings. I wondered where or how they got wings. So one warm spring morning just before I left for school, I asked, "Nonna, how do angels get their wings?"

"Angels get their wings from *you*, with God's approval. We know that angels need wings to fly to heaven and tell God what you need, to deliver your prayers, and to get His answer back to you. Your angel is with you because he needs feathers to fly, and you help him get his feathers. Now, if your angel has done a good job of helping you not sin, God rewards him with a new and strong feather.

"If someday you are alone, let yourself become calm and aware of the world around you. If you feel a breeze, it means your angel is near or has just passed by you. And if it is a strong breeze, it means your angel has just gotten a new feather and is letting you know about it. He wants to thank you for doing something good and for helping him get a new feather.

"Now, when you die and you have done many good things, your angel will have a lot of strong feathers and he will be able to lift you to heaven faster. If, on the other hand, you have not been good and your angel's wings are weak, it will take you longer to get to heaven. Be good so your angel will have strong wings."

Twenty-One

S he Never Would Believe Me

We were at war and life was tough. Most of the men in our family were in the armed services, and almost all the women were working in the factories. It was a hard and lonely time, hard to be in the military but also hard to be a civilian. We had to rely on the newsreels and the newspapers for all our news, so we were constantly full of the worry of not knowing what was happening to our loved ones.

We were given ration books and funny little red non-metallic things called "ration coins." Each family was given a certain number of books and coins with which to buy things that were also required for the war effort. Meats, sugar, bread, oil, coffee, gasoline, and rubber tires were some of the things we needed a coupon or coin to buy. There were shortages of many other things. We civilians lived simple, basic lives—almost Spartan lives—and we accepted whatever happened with no complaints.

Of all the things that were rationed, the sugar ration bothered Nonna the most, because it limited her baking birthday cakes and cookies for her family and friends. The holiday cookies around Easter and Christmas were especially important. To help Nonna, the family substituted brown sugar or syrup for their coffee and tea. This way we could keep the sugar ration stamps for her baking. Many times she would send what the family called "home front packages" to the servicemen in the family (much later I called them "CARE packages").

In addition to the rationing, President Roosevelt had asked all Americans to refrain from eating meat on Wednesdays. The whole nation complied willingly. For Catholics, who also had to abstain from eating meat on Fridays, this was an added day.

Because I was young, I adjusted happily to the rationing, but what bothered me and other young children were the air raid drills or "blackouts." These drills happened about every other week, mostly at night and without warning. Sometimes they lasted for hours. These drills seriously scared us children, because at the movies we had seen the newsreels of the bombings of London and other big cities. To think that this could happen to us scared us to prayer.

During blackouts all lights had to be out. Windows had to be covered with dark window shades. The streets were dark and abandoned; no one was permitted on them except air raid wardens. The police halted all traffic with the help of a volunteer civilian police force called the auxiliary police.

As time went on and we became more used to these drills, they became fun. We would gather in the darkness near each other and talk about family and friends. We younger ones got to know our family background through the stories Nonna would tell us. We got to know each other's likes and dislikes. We would sing in low voices, and we would joke and laugh just as quietly. Often, so very often, we would pray the Rosary.

It was during these times that Nonna was at her best. She would tell us stories about her childhood and about her family and friends in "the old country," about her two dead husbands and her courtships. We would laugh at her innocence and her ignorance of dating.

Her first marriage was arranged by her parents when she was sixteen. She had two daughters with her first husband, and then he died. Her second marriage to my grandfather was "for love," she told us, and she had two daughters and one son with him before he died. So by the time she reached twenty-six, she had been widowed two times. She decided that there was no more room in her life for men, only children, whom she raised alone.

As she told us these things, she would be crocheting. She never dropped a stitch or made a mistake. My mother and aunts could not crochet in the dark during an air raid. They would have to stop and wait for the "all clear" and the lights. We grandchildren believed that crocheting in the dark was something that assuredly only Nonna could do.

Of all the air raids, the one I recall most often because of its importance is the one that took place when Nonna and I were in King of Peace Church on Holy Thursday.

Holy Thursday, the night of the Last Supper, is always a special time for devotions to Christ present in the Eucharist. It was the custom for us to visit at least three different churches on this feast day and to thank Christ for being with us until the end of time, as He promised in the Scriptures. The interior of each church was beautifully adorned with flowers and candles. That evening we made visits at two other churches near our home and finally at King of Peace.

About two minutes after we arrived, we heard the wail of the air raid sirens. Within seconds Fr. Cosago came into the church and in Italian told everyone that he would have to shut off the lights and blow out the candles. We would have to sit in the dark and wait for the "all clear." Soon Fr. Wassel and Fr. Loughery came in. The three priests huddled in deep conversation, and finally Fr. Wassel declared that they would leave some of the red vigil candles burning.

We sat with several of the nuns and other parishioners, about thirty-five of us, in near total darkness. The church was heavy with silence. Every sound, even the hushed whispering of people in prayer, could be heard almost as if it had been spoken aloud.

After about ten minutes, an old girlfriend of my grandmother announced that she was going to lead us in the Rosary. That meant that she would say the first part of the prayers and everyone else would respond with the last part. So she began the Rosary in Italian, and we all answered in Italian. I heard the Irish Nuns, who were sitting directly in front of us, responding in English. Hearing the responses in both languages made me giggle a little, until Nonna nudged me. "Don't you see and feel the beauty of what is happening? God hears all prayers no matter what language we speak," she said in a whisper.

Within fifteen minutes the Rosary was over, and we again sat in silence. I watched the magic of the flickering candles as they danced around the ceiling and walls of the church, and I began to see the beauty of silence.

The candles also reflected off the tall statues of the saints, making the statues appear to be moving. I became frightened by this phenomenon, because I didn't want God or any of His friends to talk to me or to appear to me. I would not know what to do with such an important event as that. I quickly closed my eyes and began to think of other things. Soon I was thinking of how great it would have been to be at the first Last Supper.

"Nonna," I whispered, "did you ever wish you were at the Last Supper?"

She looked down at me. Her face looked very strange in the semi-darkness, and I wondered if my face looked as strange to her.

She smiled, "But I was there."

"Nonna!" I exclaimed loudly, thereby drawing attention to us both.

When everyone stopped looking at us, Nonna looked at me with her mouth covered. I knew she was giggling. After a few more moments she looked again at me.

"This is a good place to tell this story," she said in a voice just above a whisper. I was certain those around us were able to hear. "It is Holy Thursday, so it is good.

"Just before St. Mark left for his travels with St. Paul, he went to see St. Joseph of Arimathea. He gave Joseph a small package and told him to hold it until he came back. Joseph asked him what the package contained, and St. Mark told him that it was the cup that Jesus drank from at the Last Supper. It had been left at his mother's house, the place of the Last Supper, and it was too important a cup to leave there.

"St. Joseph became very excited. He carefully held the package close to his chest as he walked to his house. He had long envied the apostles for their privilege of sharing the Last Supper with Jesus and had often wished that he had been a part of that night. When he arrived at his house, he placed the package on the kitchen table and unwrapped it. A bright, blinding light surrounded the cup, and Joseph fell to his knees in adoration and prayer.

"When he finally had the courage to look up, the light was gone. He stood up and went to the cup with the idea of rewrapping it and hiding it in a safe place. But as he looked inside the cup, he saw it was full of the Blood of Jesus under the appearance of wine.

"He then heard a familiar Voice say, 'Joseph, take and drink, this is My Blood.'

"Joseph obeyed happily. From that day on, St. Joseph felt he had been a part of the Last Supper. He hid the cup safely away, so safely that it has never been found and never will be found, because now God makes every cup used at Mass the cup of the Last Supper. So we, like Joseph, are part of the Last Supper. Do you understand now why I say I was there?"

I nodded my head, understanding that I also had been at the Last Supper many times.

The "all clear" shrilled, and moments later the church lights came on and people began to leave quietly. Sr. Mary Evangeline, the eighth-grade teacher, leaned over the pew and whispered in Italian to my grandmother, "That was a beautiful story. Did you hear that when you were a child in Italy?"

"No, Sister," Nonna said, "I just thought of it."

"That was beautiful," Sister said. She looked at me. "You go to our school, don't you?"

"Yes, Sister," I replied respectfully.

"What grade are you in?"

"Second grade."

"Oh, yes, Sr. Mary Killian's class," she said smiling. She looked at my grandmother and in Italian said, "Have a Happy Easter."

"Happy Easter," we replied.

Sister filed quietly out of the pew and, with the other nuns, out of the church. Then we walked out.

Early on the morning of the first day after our Easter break, Sr. Mary Killian told me to report to Sr. Mary Evangeline's class. When I arrived at the eighth-grade room, Sister put me in front of her students and told me to repeat the story Nonna had told me on Holy Thursday. I retold the story, wondering why I was doing it. The next day I had to repeat the story to my classmates and before long to many other classrooms in my school.

When I told Nonna what I had been doing in school, she laughed and told me to stop fibbing and teasing her. She didn't believe me.

Many years later some of the nuns from the school were at Nonna's funeral Mass. One, Sr. Mary Thaddeus, walked over to me and told me that many of the Sisters who had taught at our school and had been transferred to other schools throughout the States had repeated my grandmother's Holy Thursday story to their students.

"Vincent, you should be proud of your grandmother, because she is a famous storyteller," Sister said to me.

"I know, Sister," I told her. "But if I had told Nonna she was that, she never would believe me."

"Maybe now she knows," Sister said softly.

Twenty-Two

A Day to Remember

It was June 6, 1944.

I don't remember the proper sequence to that day, but I do remember many things about it. It was a few days before the end of school. It was a time of relief because all our Archdiocesan Examinations were completed. All the students in Catholic schools waited anxiously for their final grades.

I remember Nonna telling me, "Vinzee, remember this day. History is being made, and you are living through an important day in history."

I remember seeing the dining room table covered with small and large burning vigil candles. It was never a surprise to see a vigil candle burning on this table; it was Nonna's way of appealing to God for guidance and help. Throughout the year, if there ever was a big thunderstorm or a heavy snowstorm and any member of the household was not home from work, Nonna would burn her vigil candle until the wayward member of the family had arrived safely home. Vigil candles were also burned when it was the anniversary of the death of a family member or friend. On those days there were one or two candles.

But on D-Day there were many candles. I remember sitting at the table, later that day, naming each candle for one of

Nonna's sons, sons-in-law, or nephews who was away in combat.

I remember hearing Nonna hissing and whispering early that morning. Her brow was wrinkled, and her face stone serious. I remember seeing the Rosary in her hand and more hissing and more whispering.

"Today all the churches will be crowded, and heaven will be bombarded with pleas and cries for help and protection," she said to me.

I remember the stillness and silence of the streets of Philadelphia. No horns were blowing, no trolley car bells clanking, and no people shouting. Not even any loud talking—it was all so eerie. The whole city was whispering.

I remember our school lot not being so noisy. Kids were standing and talking quietly in small groups. Mother Mary Edward's hand bell, which rang for our assembly, sounded softer and definitely was not as long as other days.

My teacher, Sr. Mary Eulalia, was very serious that day. Her face was white and without her usual big Irish smile. She looked concerned. She asked all those who had fathers, brothers, uncles, or cousins in the Armed Services to stand up. The entire class stood. Her eyes surveyed our faces, and I am sure she saw the concern, the fear, and the anxiety on all of them. She led us in a very long prayer, and when we sat down she began telling us of what an important day we were living through. Our concerns, fears, and anxieties grew more intense.

Soon one of the eighth graders entered the room. This usually meant a written note from Mother Mary Edward, our principal. Sister read the note silently. The eighth grader left the room and Sister announced that we would now go to our parish church for Benediction and prayers. After church we were to go home immediately and be with our families.

"This is a day for families to be with each other," Sister said. "The other Sisters and I will be in the convent chapel all day praying for you and your families."

We marched quietly to church, which we found crowded with more people than usual. Later I heard that all churches were open that day and that all were crowded.

I saw many of my relatives—Nonna was there—and many, many of our neighbors, male and female. I remember wondering how they knew the nuns were going to take us to church. Nonna was right; heaven was being bombarded with prayers.

As I walked home afterward, I heard radios playing loudly in the streets. President Roosevelt was speaking to the nation. The strength, rhythm, and accent of his voice echoed in my ears long after he was finished speaking. I promised myself to remember what was happening.

When I got home I went immediately to Nonna's side. She was still in prayer, and my entrance into the kitchen didn't break her thoughts or her meditation. I went to the cabinet, got the can of coffee and the coffeepot, and began to make coffee. I silently set the table for us both.

While I made the "best coffee in the world," I began to wish I could be in that far-off place called Normandy. I would love to see what was happening. This waiting, this tension, this anxiety, and this not knowing were very, very hard to endure.

"I wish I was there," I said. "I would love to see what is happening."

"God forbid!" Nonna shot back. "Can't you imagine what it would look like?" She closed her eyes and envisioned the carnage. "God forbid," she repeated softly.

I poured the coffee and sat down.

My thoughts went back to the time when we received news of the invasion of Italy. Nonna and my other relatives who had immigrated to the United States were deeply disturbed. Italy was their homeland, the place of their birth, and there was still family there.

My Uncle Tony, Nonna's brother, had told me that some Italians felt the Italian Americans had betrayed Italy because their sons were fighting in Italy. But he added in his usual tough voice, "Not me! I have a son-in-law in Italy fighting Germans. He happens to be an American who speaks Italian. He is fighting the Germans for Italy and America."

But the Italian invasion was not comparable to the massive invasion of Normandy. Normandy, we suspected, had more of our family members involved. Three weeks after the invasion our suspicions were proven correct. We had lost three family members at Normandy, and three others were wounded.

"Sometimes it is not good to see all things. Sometimes God spares us the details," Nonna said.

She told me a story that day—not in her usual way with dialogue and details—just a story:

"When Joseph and Mary finally found Jesus in the temple and He said to them, 'Did you not know I was about My Father's business?' Mary and Joseph kind of understood what He meant. But Joseph felt a great sorrow, for he knew he had lost his 'borrowed' Son and that Jesus had gone back to His heavenly Father.

"Later that same day when Mary was busy with other things,

Jesus asked Joseph to take Him for a walk. He led Joseph through the streets of Jerusalem and pointed out the people who would be at His crucifixion. He showed Joseph the place of the Last Supper. They walked to the Garden of Gethsemane, and Jesus pointed out the very spot of His betrayal. They walked on, and He pointed to where He would be beaten and crowned.

"They walked through the narrow cobbled streets, and Joseph heard about the African man who would help Him with His cross and the places He would fall. Jesus showed Joseph a young boy, a citizen of Jerusalem, who would, after he grew up, hit Jesus so hard across His face that His nose would bleed. He showed him some young boys who were passing by with their fathers who would grow up to be His apostles and some of His other followers. Together they climbed the small hill called Calvary, where Jesus would die on the cross.

"Jesus told Joseph that he would not live to see all these things, that his time, his purpose in life, would be completed before these happenings. Joseph became very distressed and pleaded with Jesus to intercede to the Father. Nothing could be done. These sights were not for Joseph.

"Jesus and Joseph returned to Mary, and when she saw them she immediately knew something was wrong. Joseph walked quickly to her and held her in his arms. He whispered in her ear, 'Mary, I will always be with you.'

"When Jesus died, the first thing He had to do was go to that place where all the people who had prepared His way were. Abraham, Moses, David, Daniel, Job, and many more greeted Him. But He was looking only for Joseph, whom He saw all the way in the back. Jesus walked to him, they embraced, and Jesus said to him, 'Mother knew you were with her. More importantly, I knew you were there. I heard your sobs and your prayers.'"

I remember after the story timidly asking, "Wasn't it worse for Joseph not to be there?"

Nonna waited a long time and replied, "Yes, I guess so, but at least he was spared the sights and sounds of it all. It is the gift of sparing. It is a small gift, and it is a generous gift from a generous God."

Years later, when I studied all the things that went wrong or could have gone wrong with the invasion of Normandy, I realized how wise Nonna was. I also realized how all our thoughts, candles, and prayers helped.

It *was* a day to remember.

$\mathcal{H}$ow Rich We All Are!

Nonna often told me that I was going to grow up and get rich and take care of her. I believed this because she never was wrong. I truly believed that God wanted me to do this.

After all, she had had a hard life. In her old age I wanted her to have the good things she deserved.

One day, I cannot remember why, she began to tell me this story. At the time I did not understand it, but years later I did.

A great and well-venerated Italian saint once wrote a story about getting old, getting rich, and taking care of your loved ones. The story he wrote has been handed down for many centuries in Italy and throughout Europe.

It appears that a few days after Jesus ascended into heaven, the apostles were deep in prayer. They were still at St. Mark's house, still not too sure of themselves. Now, of course, we all know that they were waiting for the Holy Spirit.

One day Peter said that he believed the Scriptures had to be fulfilled and someone must be chosen to take the place of Judas. All agreed.

"But," Peter said, "before this can happen, we must find out where Judas is." All agreed. So Mark was sent with a message to Nicodemus and Joseph of Arimathea, asking them once again to use their good offices to find out what had happened to Judas.

The next night, in secrecy, Nicodemus and Joseph the Arimathean came to Mark's house and the upper room where the apostles were staying. They told the apostles that Judas had hung himself. His body had been placed in a new graveyard outside the city walls, called the "Field of Blood."

Much to everyone's surprise, Peter said he wanted to go to the grave. Everyone tried to talk Peter out of this insane idea, but Peter was bullheaded and said that it had to be done. In fact, he insisted that they all had to go. So late the next day the apostles secretly left the upper room two by two, and they assembled at a seldom-visited patch of forest just outside the city walls. Then Joseph of Arimethea led them to the grave of Judas.

As the Twelve approached the grave, several of them were filled with sadness. Six of them stopped on the roadside and watched as the other five—Peter, John, Thomas, Simon the Zealot, and Matthew—walked closer. A quarter of the way to the grave Thomas stopped—then Matthew, then John, and finally the Zealot. Peter continued on until he stood before the grave. He began to sob. Tears streamed down his face. Those on the roadside were shocked to see this, but those who had walked closer to the grave with Peter understood.

They heard Peter say, "Judas, it could have been me."

Softly, one by one, those nearest Peter whispered in agreement and acknowledgment, "Or me." Just then from out of nowhere came a man. He was racing quickly, excitedly toward the scared band of men.

"Sir," he shouted loudly.

Peter was startled and immediately drew his robe up to his face. He was trying to hide himself. The others who were standing nearby stepped back in fear and quickly drew their cloaks up to their faces.

The third group of apostles, those standing watch on the road, began to move further away.

"Oh, please, sir, help me," said the stranger loudly.

"What is it you want of me?" Peter asked.

"Did you know this man? This man who lies here in this unmarked grave?"

Peter's mind returned to the night of Jesus' arrest. Again he saw the large fire, felt its heat on his face, and heard the questions of the servants. There can be no more denials, he thought.

"Yes," he said in a low, controlled voice.

"Thank God. I have been looking for some of His companions."

"Why do you seek them?" Peter inquired carefully.

"I have wanted to talk, just talk. Can I speak to you, sir?"

"Yes," replied Peter.

"The day of that man Jesus' trial I could not find a place of refuge. I wanted so to hide, but no matter where I ran, I saw Golgatha—that damned hill. Even when I closed my eyes, I saw the hill and on it the three crosses. There was no getting away from it. So I ran and ran and ran, blindly.

"After a while I realized that I would never be able to run away from that hill. I have been tortured with guilt. Guilt has called me back to that hill, for I should have been there. The more I ran, the more I became aware that I was guilty of deserting this man Jesus. Then this man," he pointed to Judas' grave, "came upon me.

"He was in worse shape than I was. He was shouting and cursing himself and the womb that bore him. He cursed his father, his mother, and all his family. He shouted to me, 'Stay clear of me, for I have killed the Son of God. I have betrayed life itself! Love itself! All of the loneliest moments of the universe have come to rest on me. Stay clear!'

"'But, sir,' I yelled back to him, 'I am like you, and I need to help someone. Please, let me help you.'

"'I am beyond all help, but go tell the others. Go tell Jesus' followers that they are to help you. They will make you understand. Tell them that they are the richest of all people, for God will hear their voices. Now leave me! Leave me to my hells.'

"With those words he ran up the nearby hillside and vanished. It was then that the day changed to night and all earth vomited its anger on us. Do you remember the darkness? And the quakes? And the wind? God, what a day it became! Never have I seen such anger.

"Two days later I came upon Romans removing the body of this man," again he pointed to the grave, "from a tree. He had killed himself. As they passed by my hiding place, I remembered what this man had said and began to seek you out. I went to the place where I heard they had buried Jesus. I wanted to go and ask forgiveness for what had happened. When I saw the guards at the tomb, I again ran and I again tried to find you. Finally I decided to hide here, assured that you would come to see this grave."

The apostles by now had all grouped near Peter. They realized that this man who was speaking was of no harm to them.

"You have suffered much, brother. What can we do for you?"

"Tell me, what did this Man mean? Tell me, what do I need to know from you about this Man Jesus?" The stranger fell to his knees and began to cry. "This Jesus, He saved me. He gave me new life. He suffered and died for me."

"Did you ever see or hear Jesus speak?" asked Philip.

"Once. Briefly," the man sobbed, still on his knees.

"I know this man," announced Simon the Zealot.

"And I also," added John.

"Who are you?" asked Matthew.

"I am called Barabbas," said the stranger. "I am the one who was chosen to live. I am he for whom your Jesus died." He slowly rose to his feet. "Could it be, good sirs, that this good and just Man, this holy Man, came to life to die for me so that I may live?"

"The answer to that question, dear Barabbas, is not for us to answer," Peter said, reaching out for Barabbas' hand. "It is something you and we must seek together. We must hope and pray for help from the One who has created these questions within us, that He will make us find the answers in our prayers."

"But who was this man?" Barabbas asked, pointing to the grave.

"He was the betrayer of Jesus," stated Peter. "And I am he who denied Jesus three times." He immediately fell into deep thought and sorrow.

"And I am he who deserted Him, for I could have defended Him to the death," said Barabbas.

James son of Zebedee stepped forward, embraced Barabbas, and said, "And so are we all deserters, for we also ran from Him."

"And here we all stand at the grave of the one who was one of us," said James son of Alphaeus. "And poor Judas said we were the richest of all people. How are we to come to terms with this statement?"

"Perhaps we are the richest because we can do the only thing He cannot do," stated Andrew. "We can help him with our prayers; we can ask mercy for him."

"I believe Andrew is right," Peter announced, and the others all murmured in agreement.

Peter reached for Barabbas and embraced him.

"Come, Barabbas, Robber of Life, come with us, and we will see what God wants us to find," said Peter. "Let us go, to learn to pray and to give away our treasure of riches."

And so they all returned to Mark's house, to the upper room, and prayed for those who were poorer than they were.

Several years later Nonna became sick with cancer.

I often would sit with her, and we would just talk of old days and old things. They were good talks. When it became obvious to me that she was suffering a great deal and was dying, the dream of growing up, getting rich, and tending to her also began to die.

On one of the worst nights of her pain, I went into her bedroom. I wanted so to help her with her suffering. We tried to talk, but the pain distracted her thoughts. Finally I said I was sorry, but I did not think I would be able to take care of her in her old age. I still remember how hard a thing this was for me to say. I fought back the tears that wanted and needed to be shed.

She smiled, squeezed my hand weakly, and began to mumble

something. I leaned over close to her lips and heard her say in Italian, "You will.... You are rich in prayers.... You will pray for me.... Take care of me now, Vinzee. Pray extra hard tonight."

That night I prayed for my Nonna. I prayed that God would stop the pain, even if it meant taking her from our family. I promised that I would accept His will knowing it will be hard to do. Nonna died during the night.

Several years after Nonna's death I went to visit her grave with my father. I thought of the story of Barabbas and saw all the years that I had taken care of her in her death. All the years I had prayed for her. I realized how rich I would always be, for I would have many, many more years to pray for her.

I was grown up and rich and tending to her in her new life.